SAMURAI

馬渡防牛

Stephen Turnbull

SAMURAI

The Japanese Warrior's (Unofficial) Manual

126 illustrations, 15 in color

Thames & Hudson

For Ian Clark – who else?

Stephen Turnbull is Lecturer on Japanese Religion at Leeds University and also holds
the post of Visiting Professor of Japanese Studies at Akita International University in
Japan. He has two MAs (in Military History and in Theology) and a PhD for his work
on Japanese religion. His seventy published books include *The Samurai: A Military
History*, *Samurai: The World of the Warrior* and *The Revenge of the 47 Ronin, Edo 1703*.
He acted as Historical Advisor for Universal Pictures for the 2012 movie *47 Ronin*,
starring Keanu Reeves.

COVER *A samurai commander signals with his war fan.*
HALF-TITLE *The hollyhock-leaves mon (a badge or family crest)
of the Tokugawa shoguns.*
TITLE PAGE *Lord Umawatari Bogyu working on another masterpiece,
in the days before he shaved his head and became a follower of Pure
Land Buddhism.*

First published in 2012 in hardcover in the United States
of America by Thames & Hudson Inc., 500 Fifth Avenue,
New York, New York 10110

thamesandhudsonusa.com

Library of Congress Catalog Card Number 2011935883

ISBN 978-0-500-25188-1

Text pages designed and typeset by Fred Birdsall studio
Printed and bound in China by Toppan Leefung

Contents

The audience for Lord Umawatari Bogyu's book was the young untrained
samurai who would develop into this man: the peerless samurai warrior,
accomplished in the arts of war and peace, brave on the battlefield,
wise in his judgments and loyal to the point of death.

Samurai

The Japanese Warrior's (Unofficial) Manual and its author: Umawatari Bogyu

S *amurai: The Japanese Warrior's (Unofficial) Manual,* originally en-titled *Buke Monogatari* (literally 'Tales of the Military Class') is the masterpiece of samurai instruction compiled in 1615 by Umawatari Bogyu (1549–1615), the lord of Hitachi province in northeastern Japan. Bogyu was a renowned samurai warrior who held the position of grand chamberlain to Tokugawa Hidetada (1579–1632), the shogun (military dictator) commissioned by the divine emperor to rule Japan on his behalf.

Bogyu (the name Lord Umawatari took on becoming a Buddhist monk in 1611) was the younger brother of Honda Tadakatsu (1548–1610), one of the greatest samurai of the 16th century. Although Bogyu had been adopted into the Umawatari family in 1560 when the previous Umawatari lord died childless, he continued to serve the Tokugawa family as his Honda ancestors had done for centuries. He fought loyally for Tokugawa Ieyasu (1543–1616) at Nagakute (1584), Odawara (1590) and the decisive battle of Sekigahara in 1600, after which his master re-established the historic position of shogun. As a reward for his service at Sekigahara, Lord Umawatari was given the rich domain of Hitachi province, and in 1611 he was appointed grand chamberlain to the second shogun, Tokugawa Hidetada, who took over from his illustrious father Ieyasu when the latter abdicated in 1605. In 1615, while the fierce Osaka campaign was still at its height, the shogun commissioned Bogyu to compile *Buke Monogatari* for the education of his young samurai, and even supplied a foreword for the work – an unprecedented honour that reflected the great importance the government attached to this unique book.

Foreword

by His Most Excellent Highness
Lord Tokugawa Hidetada,
Shogun of Japan

✝ ✝ ✝

So, young man, you want to be a samurai? Does that question surprise you? Am I suggesting that you were born a farmer or a merchant? Of course not! Be reassured by Our Own Most Excellent Person that you are already a samurai, having been born into that most glorious social class. To be a samurai is your birthright, and none can deprive you of it.

No, the purpose of this book, which we have seen fit to commission from the brush of our grand chamberlain, is to assist a young samurai to transform himself from being merely the fortunate occupant of an exalted social position into a true samurai warrior: fearless on the battlefield; accomplished in the arts of war and peace; wise in administration; an example to the lower orders; and one who will bring honour to his ancestors.

So why have we commissioned this work at this particular time in our country's illustrious history? Are we not presently living in the Age of Maitreya (The Buddha Who Is To Come), where peace and plenty have been showered upon us owing to the virtues and wisdom of My Most Illustrious Father? Indeed we are. In this First Year of the Year Period of Genna – being the Fifth Year of the Reign of The Imperial Son of Heaven His Divine Majesty Emperor Gomizuno-o and the two thousand, two hundred and seventy-fifth year since the accession of Jimmu, the first emperor of Japan, which, using the Chinese calendar, is the Year of the Hare and Junior Brother of the Wood – we are blessed indeed.

Take note, however, that it is our sincere wish that henceforth in this book all dates should be rendered after the manner of the barbarians who arrived from the south. Why, I hear you ask, should we have chosen to do something so unspeakably vulgar? We reply that it is our wish that this book should be read not only by young samurai such as yourself, but also circulated abroad among the barbarian nations, so that they may know the martial virtues and military glories of our land, and tremble thereat.

By such vulgar barbarian reckoning it is now the year 1615, and my heart swells with pride when I contemplate the fact that my own beloved son and heir, Tokugawa Iemitsu, has lived within the radiant glory of the Tokugawa family for 15 years. Indeed it was on an auspicious day in the year 1600 that My Most Illustrious Father vanquished upon the bloody field of Sekigahara those who were so misguided as to deny his all-encompassing virtue. My Most Illustrious Father consequently re-established the post of shogun that – because of the actions of sinful men – had fallen so grievously into abeyance, thus bringing peace to our realm, leading our armies to victory and spreading his wisdom and virtue to the far seas. I have continued his task as best I can, and when the time comes for me to depart this life and join My Most Excellent Father as a Guest in the White Jade Pavilion, my beloved son Iemitsu will succeed to the position of shogun, and continue our illustrious work.

So study this book, young man, and devote yourself to it, for much remains to be done. A cruel winter has just passed, during which our benevolent rule was most unwisely challenged by a rabble of enemies confined within the mighty walls of Osaka Castle. Owing to the martial glory of My Most Illustrious Father, peace has been restored, yet even as I write there are rumours that those same rebels have seen fit to re-excavate the moats of Osaka, which we, in our infinite mercy, caused to be filled in using the walls of the very same castle. So once again the martial hosts of the Tokugawa family, assisted most loyally by the samurai of the great lords of Japan whose love and filial piety towards us knows no end, must assemble for a final chastisement.

Read this book, young man, and you may take your place on the battlefield of Osaka as a true samurai!

May the gods and Buddhas take heed, and may they blast all transgressors!

Hidetada

Preface

by Umawatari Bogyu,
Lord of Hitachi and Grand Chamberlain to
His Most Excellent Highness the Shogun

✛ ✛ ✛

As a person of no consequence, to have received a commission from His Most Excellent Highness the Shogun Lord Tokugawa Hidetada to compile this book, it was as if the sun in heaven had set in one's dustbin. That His Most Excellent Highness should then see fit to write a foreword to this miserable wretch's unworthy work is to be likened to a dragon shedding its scales above a dung-heap. Compared to the exquisiteness of His Most Excellent Highness's delicate calligraphy, the scribbling from the ink-brush of this person of no regard may be likened to a dog leaving scratch marks on a garden fence. For this worm-like creature to expound upon military matters from within the shadow cast by the martial glory of His Most Excellent Highness is to liken the divine fury of the Four Guardian Kings of Heaven to a sardine gnashing its teeth. To compare my pitiful and inadequate observations on the business of government to those of His Most Excellent Highness would be to liken the fierce breaths of a warhorse to a night-soil collector's nag breaking wind.

I therefore submit the following unworthy observations in an attitude of profound respect, immense gratitude and utter humility.

Bogyu

1
Japan Today – What Every Samurai Needs to Know

The special dispensation of our Imperial Land means that ours is the native land of the Heaven-Shining Goddess who casts her light over all countries in the four seas. Thus our country is the source and fountainhead of all other countries, and in all matters it excels all the others.

MOTOORI NORINAGA, ON THE EMPEROR AND JAPAN

Why Our Nation is Superior to All Others

Japan is the Land of the Gods, uniquely favoured by Heaven above all other nations. Later in this book you will read of these kami (gods) and the many blessings they have bestowed upon us, among which, of course, is the great treasure-house of martial virtue as exemplified by samurai like you. Is it not by the swords of the samurai that we are known and feared? Indeed it is, but in addition to the knowledge of our virtues spreading across the seas, our land is uniquely favoured by good government.

All this is due to the Will of Heaven, a fact that may be readily appreciated by comparing the favourable situation Japan enjoys to the position of the celestial kingdom of China. Her emperors have received from Heaven a divine mandate to rule, but it is a mandate that can be removed from them at any time. Thus the dynasty of the Tang was replaced by that of the Song, and the Song by that of the Yuan, and the Yuan by the Ming who currently reign; even the glorious Ming may one day have Heaven's mandate taken from them. Not so Japan, for Heaven bestowed upon our first emperor an everlasting mandate, and it is his family that reigns now and will do so forever.

But Japan is twice blessed, for it was the will of a certain emperor many centuries ago to pass on this great burden of kingship to a superlative samurai called Minamoto Yoritomo, giving him the title of shogun. Yoritomo was a man who, by the exercise of his virtue and military glory, had ensured that Japan was at peace. He was the first shogun, and His Most Excellent Highness Tokugawa Hidetada is the present incumbent of that illustrious office. When you are grown to manhood you will be part of his great government, and will occupy some small but important position in the great chain of loyalty and benevolence by which Japan is ruled so wisely and so well.

Emperor Go-Uda, who was reigning at the time of the Mongol Invasions of the 13th century, a glorious period in samurai history when the various clans stood united as never before. It was only on occasions such as this that an emperor became memorable.

How shall I illustrate this great chain of harmony? Think if you will of the peerless Mount Fuji, the perfect cone of which enchants the eyes of all who see it. Imagine that Fuji is Japan itself, and that those who rule our land are seated thereon. On the summit sits the emperor of Japan. None is nearer to Heaven than he, and this is rightly so, for he is heaven-descended. Myriad years ago, Amaterasu (the Goddess of the Sun, whose life-giving radiance fills all) sent her descendant to earth to become our first emperor, and from him succeeds in an unbroken line His Divine Majesty The Emperor Gomizuno-o – whose own radiance presently illuminates us.

But see, young samurai, there is one seated beside him who, at the emperor's behest, rules this land so that the Divine Son of Heaven may exercise his superior virtue unhindered by the tedious business of government. This is our shogun. Alas, for many years there was no shogun because of the actions of sinful men, but within my own most happy lifetime the position was restored by His Most Illustrious Highness Lord Tokugawa Ieyasu, and it is his son, His Most Excellent Highness Lord Tokugawa Hidetada, whom you now see seated beside the emperor.

You will also see that around these two illustrious figures sit many in court robes, serving them in innumerable ways. These men are wise counsellors, scholars and administrators, who belong to the families of the emperor and the shogun. Now look below these imperial servants, for stretched out in their countless thousands are men such as you – the samurai of Japan. So multitudinous are they that the slopes of Mount Fuji are rendered invisible by their glittering host. Our eyes move further downwards, and thousands more people are seen. Their appearance is vulgar but their toil is honourable: they are the farmers, whose blessed role it is to grow the rice, which is itself a divine gift.

A samurai shown indoors, seated and holding his fan. He wears only the shorter sword (wakizashi), his longer katana having been deposited at the door. This is a necessary courtesy required by one's host.

- - - - - - - - - - - - - -

14

And now we see a further ring of people. Their appearance is not rough, for many wear fine silks, but their trade is vulgar: these are the merchants who engage in commerce. From this, many have grown so rich that their wealth may exceed that of noble samurai, whose treasure, of course, lies not in gold. Within their ranks may be noted honoured craftsmen who forge swords or carve ivory, who paint scrolls or print books. That such beauty may come from people so coarse! It is a mystery indeed!

Below them we have a ring of diverse people whose position in society places them upon the lower slopes. Here may be found actors, singers, puppeteers, conjurers, dancers and other sordid persons. Yet among them walk doctors and priests, who are men of virtue and learning. Had Heaven blessed them with higher birth they might well be listed among the number of the samurai. Alas for them, it was not to be.

Finally, scurrying betwixt the throngs and despised by them are the lowest of the low. These people are scarcely human because their trade is with filth and with animals. They kill beasts and make leather. They also execute criminals and dispose of corpses. Such people are to be shunned, as are the beggars, the murderers and the outcasts who also hide in the shadows, unenlightened by the radiance flowing from the great mountain's peak.

Two coopers making a large wooden sake barrel. This is a task typical of the craftsmen and merchants who live in castle-towns in a social position vastly inferior to that of the samurai.

Thus it is that the benevolence of the great is passed down to the vulgar, and the loyalty of the sordid is passed upwards to the good. So it was written by the sage Confucius, who saw that the government of men must be harmonious, and that harmony could only be achieved in this manner. Wherever a man has been born on this mountain, there he will surely stay. You, young man, are blessed to have been born a samurai, and so you will serve those above and rule those beneath, displaying the virtue that has been bestowed upon you.

A History of Japan to the Present Happy Time

As noted above by His Most Excellent Highness, we are indeed living in an age of peace and plenty, where the mountains spew forth gold and supplicant barbarians vie with each other to lay their tribute at our feet. Yet this most blessed and auspicious situation was achieved only at the cost of the blood of the samurai, to whose ranks you now aspire. I most unworthily begin this book by presenting an account of how the samurai of the Tokugawa family triumphed over their foes to make Japan what it is today.

Many years ago the words 'samurai' and 'shogun' were both unknown. In those unenlightened times the emperors, taking their cue most unwisely from the example set by the Tang dynasty of China, decided that peace within their realm could be attained by fielding an army consisting of conscripted peasants. How misguided they were! As a result the city of Nara, created the first permanent capital of Japan in the year 710, became the target of rebels and malcontents, while our borders were threatened by hordes of barbarians from across the seas. How fortunate it was for these early emperors that there also existed in Japan proud families who, by the sweat of their own labour, had caused rice fields to flourish in lands thought inhospitable, and had favoured commerce and industry within their own modest estates. These land-owners, being faced with understandable jealousy from neighbours, had been forced to resort to arms to defend their territories, thereby waxing strong in the martial virtues. In an act of unparalleled loyalty and generosity towards the Imperial Son of Heaven, these same land-owners most kindly made available to the imperial household their own armies of fierce warriors, whom they called 'those who serve' – i.e. 'samurai'. Thus did samurai become servants of the emperor; vanquishing his rebels, securing his borders and covering themselves in martial glory.

Alas, in the year 1160 Lord Taira Kiyomori, a samurai leader of much valour, became overcome by overweening pride and sought power for his own selfish ends. By marrying his daughter into the imperial line,

Kiyomori took the reins of power into his own hands and ruled from behind the throne as imperial grandfather. Fortunately for Japan, there was in the north of our land one other family of great military skill and accomplished martial virtue. This was the family of Minamoto, from whom His Most Excellent Highness is descended. The Minamoto arose and chastised the Taira in a long and bitter conflict known as the Gempei War, which lasted from 1180 to 1185. The emperor, whose gratitude towards the Minamoto was profound, begged their leader Yoritomo to accept the title of shogun. Being a modest man, Yoritomo of course wished to decline this unprecedented honour, but saw that it was his duty to accept the wishes of His Divine Majesty the Emperor and humbly agreed.

Thus it was that the first shogun of Japan began to rule in the name of the emperor. Woe, within three generations the Minamoto fell foul of scheming by rivals from the Hojo family, and the bakufu (shogunate) fell temporarily into disuse. Without a shogun's benevolence, Japan lay open to attack from barbarians, who appeared on our shores in 1274. These were armies of Mongol warriors from the vast plains of Asia, sent by Kublai Khan, a rude nomadic barbarian who had seized the dragon throne of the emperors of China. Japan was attacked and our brave samurai were bombarded most cruelly with exploding devices and poisoned arrows. Fighting back, they drove away the invaders only to have them return seven years later with a new army as numerous as grains of sand on a seashore. Yet once again, the barbarians were repulsed by the heroism of our samurai warriors, and were then utterly destroyed by the kamikaze – a wind sent from the gods. This miraculous typhoon sank their fleet (completing what our army's valour had already begun) and was a direct result of the prayers and petitions offered to the gods by the divine emperor.

Half a century later the gods rewarded the emperor still further by arranging a grand chastisement of the usurpers of the shogunate. In the year 1333, numerous valiant warriors arose to vanquish the Hojo rebels at His Majesty's bidding. One among their number, Ashikaga Takauji, of the line of the Minamoto, was then requested by His Majesty to accept the vacant title of shogun. Being a modest man, Takauji of course wished to decline this great honour, but (as you may have guessed) saw that it was his duty to accept the wishes of His Divine Majesty the Emperor, and humbly agreed.

Two boatloads of samurai are rowed out to attack the Mongol fleet as it lies at anchor in Hakata Bay during the second Mongol invasion, which took place in 1281. Few events in Japanese history were more honourable than the defeat of this mighty host.

Fifteen members of the Ashikaga family were to be shoguns over the next two centuries, and many were the blessings we received from them. By the year 1467, however, they had grown weak and effeminate, and were unable to control the greed of rival samurai clans who disputed one with another, and Japan again fell into chaos. Samurai fought against samurai, treacherous retainers overcame their own lords, and even peasants and monks formed armies. Men who had once been farmers or had sold umbrellas now styled themselves daimyo, meaning lords, and built castles on mountains to defend their petty territories, thus disrupting the natural order of things. So terrible was the time that it became known as the Age of Warring States. The land yearned for peace, but worse was to come.

The Ashikaga family had become so weak that when barbarians from Europe arrived in Japan in 1543 to enslave the people with their false treasures and their pernicious religion of Christianity there was none who dared oppose them. No kamikaze typhoon blew to sink the black ships of the Southern Barbarians. Instead, certain unscrupulous lords, who had been enticed and blinded by the wealth in silks and exotic goods brought by these wicked European strangers, began to trade with them. Some of these Japanese lords were so misguided that they even abandoned the gods of Japan and accepted the evil and disruptive doctrines of Christianity. These traitors grew rich both in gold and in the means of war, for the Southern Barbarians had also brought with them guns – weapons that had never before been seen in Japan.

A samurai in the civilian dress of hakama trousers and haori jacket, still wearing the two swords that are the hallmark of the samurai class. He has a typical fashionable hairstyle.

- - - - - - -

Now, as you will clearly appreciate, for a true samurai to fire a gun would be an act of unspeakable vulgarity. Yet many succumbed to the temptation, and went so far as to give guns to peasants whom they placed in the front ranks of their armies – a position that had previously been occupied only by noble samurai like you. How pitiful and tragic it was when men of breeding, accomplished in the arts of war and peace, were shot dead by these fiendish weapons fired by persons of no regard. A brave samurai – killed by a bullet from a weapon, the noise of which alone may have caused the man discharging it to run away in terror. Such ignominy!

Yet salvation was close at hand. His Most Illustrious Highness Lord Tokugawa Ieyasu (the distinguished father of our own Most Excellent Highness) was, with his wisdom and martial virtue, destined by the gods and Buddhas to restore peace and harmony throughout the land.

As a man of great modesty and piety his estates were few and his army small, so he patiently bided his time while the armies of those of overweening pride fought themselves into extinction.

Tokugawa Ieyasu, the first of the Tokugawa shoguns and the father of the second shogun, Tokugawa Hidetada.

Two great leaders then arose to begin the salvation of Japan. The first was Oda Nobunaga, Lord of Owari, at whose side His Most Illustrious Highness Lord Tokugawa Ieyasu fought most valiantly, and the second was Lord Toyotomi Hideyoshi, who avenged Oda Nobunaga when the latter was ruthlessly murdered in the year 1582. This Hideyoshi (who, unbelievably, was the son of a peasant) had been unexpectedly honoured by the gods with the gifts of martial virtue. He was defeated in battle only once, and that was at Nagakute in 1584 by His Most Illustrious Highness Lord Tokugawa Ieyasu, who, showing that mercy and generosity of spirit for which he is renowned, made alliance with him. So did their joint swords triumph, and by the year 1591 Japan was reunified once again.

Alas for Lord Toyotomi Hideyoshi, it was his fate to finally succumb to overweening pride, and in 1592 he went to war against the emperor of the great Ming. Many thousands of samurai landed in Korea and began to fight their way towards Beijing, a task they never accomplished. His Most Illustrious Highness Lord Tokugawa Ieyasu foresaw the folly inherent in such a scheme, and wisely declined to send his samurai to China. Other lords complied with the foolishness of Hideyoshi and suffered as a result. When the defeated Japanese army returned from the Korean peninsula they found Lord Toyotomi Hideyoshi dead of madness.

Toyotomi Hideyoshi, who rose from being the son of a foot soldier to rule the whole of Japan. He secured the reunification of the country in 1591 following a series of brilliant military campaigns.

Neither Lord Toyotomi Hideyoshi nor his great predecessor Lord Oda Nobunaga, whose ancestral lineages were of unspeakable vulgarity compared to the Tokugawa family, could have taken the title of shogun, and neither had dared appropriate such an honourable position. His Divine Majesty the Emperor was in despair about whom he could choose to succeed to the position of shogun. Yet the gods took heed, and following the death of Toyotomi Hideyoshi in 1598 a miracle occurred. As the heir, Lord Toyotomi Hideyori, was a boy of five years and thus clearly unsuited to the governance of this proud land, the illustrious Lord Tokugawa Ieyasu took it upon himself to restore the harmony for which all men prayed. Sadly, there were those who did not appreciate the extent of his all-encompassing virtue, and, in the name of the child Toyotomi Hideyori, they opposed the wisdom of His Most Illustrious Highness and made war against him. In 1600 there was fought a great battle at Sekigahara, and these misguided rebels were utterly, and suitably, vanquished.

Seeing that peace had been restored to his realm owing to the martial virtue of the Tokugawa family, the emperor begged Lord Tokugawa Ieyasu to accept the position of shogun. His Most Illustrious Highness, being a man of great modesty and self-effacement, wished to decline this great honour, but (of course) saw that it was his duty to obey the imperial command, and reluctantly agreed.

That was the year 1603, since which this situation of harmony and bountiful plenty has continued. His work complete, in 1605 His Most Illustrious Highness abdicated from the position of shogun in favour of his son His Most Excellent Highness Lord Tokugawa Hidetada, beneath whose benevolence we now so happily dwell.

There remains one small hindrance to the achievement of the blissful harmony that our blessed land so fervently desires. Lord Toyotomi Hideyori, the son of Lord Toyotomi Hideyoshi (whose allies were defeated at Sekigahara, yet who most perplexingly refused to acknowledge the wisdom and necessity of removing him from office) has now ensconced himself within the walls of Osaka Castle in defiance of the all-encompassing wisdom and martial virtue of His Most Excellent Highness. Ere long, I know, he will most surely be chastised and removed from that place by noble samurai like you. Once this is done, with peace and harmony restored, who knows what further glory may be achieved by Japan and its great samurai warriors?

The Great Lords of Japan and How to Recognize Them

In Japan there are many daimyo (lords). A century ago, during the Age of Warring States, these lords fought selfishly one with another, and among the wisest decrees made by His Most Illustrious Highness

Lord Tokugawa Ieyasu on becoming shogun in 1603 was the decision to transfer almost all of these lords to the new territories where they now joyfully reside, basking in the radiance of the Tokugawa family. Peace and harmony are presently assured.

So let us begin with you. Should you not be fortunate enough to have been born into one of the closely related houses of the illustrious Tokugawa family (such as the Matsudaira of Kii or the Matsudaira of Owari), then you may have heard your lord being referred to as either a fudai or a tozama lord. What is the difference?

The difference is quite profound. If your lord is a fudai (an inner lord), then he is the fortunate descendant of someone who wisely served the Tokugawa family when His Most Illustrious Highness's kin were relatively unimportant, unbelievable as that now sounds. The tozama (outer lords), by contrast, were tardy in recognizing the wisdom and martial virtue of the Tokugawa family. Some, sad to relate, submitted to the shogun's benevolent rule only after being thoroughly chastised upon the bloody field of Sekigahara. Nowadays the fudai lords hold rich lands, while the tozama territories are confined to the furthest reaches of Japan, where the outer lords can do no harm.

Even though nearly all the great lords of Japan are now living in different provinces from the ones they once ruled, the main means of visually identifying them has remained the same. This is the mon, which is a badge or family crest, and the following illustration shows the mon of some of the most celebrated lords of Japan whose names are mentioned in this book. I include them merely as a sample of the hundreds you will encounter in your career. You will immediately recognize the three hollyhock leaves of His Most Excellent Highness's family the Tokugawa. Badges such as these will be displayed on the flags of the samurai and the armour of the foot soldiers as processions make their way along the highways of our land, and it is vital that you are able to identify them at a glance, for reasons that will now be explained.

The hollyhock-leaves mon of the Tokugawa shoguns.

The lovebirds mon of Date Masamune, whose domain of Sendai gives him the rule of much of northern Japan.

The Buddhist-wheel mon of Sakakibara Yasumasa, one of the most loyal followers of the Tokugawa.

The crossed-feathers mon of the Asano family of Hiroshima and Ako.

The three-hollyhock-leaves-on-one-stem mon of the Honda family, long-standing supporters of the Tokugawa.

The fan mon of Satake Yoshinobu, who was transferred to Kubota (Akita) following the battle of Sekigahara.

The horse-crossing-water mon of Umawatari Bogyu, grand chamberlain to the shogun, Tokugawa Hidetada.

The annulus mon of Kato Kiyomasa, keeper of Kumamoto Castle in Kyushu and a veteran of the Korean invasion.

The paulownia-tree mon used by the Ashikaga shoguns and later by Toyotomi Hideyoshi.

The horse's-bit mon of the independently minded Shimazu family of Satsuma on southern Kyushu.

The crane mon of the Nambu family, whose domain lies in Tohoku in the far north of Honshu Island.

The hat mon of the Yagyu family, who are the sword-fighting instructors to the Tokugawa shoguns.

Bowing – A Useful Guide

Today, the roads of Japan are frequently crowded by the to and fro of lords' armies leaving for, or returning from, their turn of duty in Edo. When encountering a lord of superior rank on the road, the lord of inferior rank will be required to dismount, and, with his entire host, bow deeply as the other passes. The vexed question of 'who should bow first, and how low?' is one that has plagued the organizers of troop movements for decades, so I humbly present the following handy guide to bowing. The first requirement is that of identification, and it is strongly recommended that the mounted scouts who customarily lead these processions have a list of badges with them, so as to avoid any confusion or possible bloodshed.

The general hierarchy of bowing is as follows:

1 The family of Tokugawa
2 The related families of the Tokugawa
3 The fudai lords
4 The tozama lords
5 Everybody else

A samurai bowing before a superior. Bowing is the acceptable gesture of respect.

The general rule concerning bowing is that any lords of a lower group will bow to those from a higher group, and lords within a particular group will bow to others within the same group according to their relative wealth. Wealth, as is customary, is expressed in koku – one koku being the amount of rice that is reckoned as sufficient to feed a man for one year. The second rule, of course, applies only *within* groups, because the fudai lords, as loyal followers of His Most Illustrious Highness, are men of modesty whose wealth does not necessarily reflect their exalted status. They therefore have priority over those more wealthy but less loyal. Thus the tozama family of Satake Yoshinobu (Kubota, Dewa province – 205,000 koku) will bow before the less wealthy fudai Sakai Tadatoshi (Kawagoe, Musashi province – 30,000 koku). The situation of certain lords may, however, change in the years to come owing to a promotion or a misdemeanour, so it is vital that you keep up to date on the matter.

The rear view of a samurai in civilian dress bowing from a kneeling position.

Having received a bow from an inferior, the superior lord must acknowledge the fact by returning a bow in recognition of the honour, making sure that his bow passes through a smaller angle of bodily declination than the salutation he has received. When the social gulf due to rank and wealth is considerable, the smallest lowering of the head in acknowledgment is more than adequate as a courtesy.

Needless to say, any farmer, merchant, actor or outcast who encounters a samurai entourage on the road should not merely bow, but immediately press his forehead into the mud and leave it there without sight or sound until the absence of noise indicates that the procession has passed by. The sole exception to this rule concerns priests, who, having bowed appropriately from the waist, may return to a vertical yet respectful position to bestow their prayers and blessings upon the passing martial host.

Those who are scarcely human – criminals and the like – must take pains to ensure that they are not even present when a lord passes, lest the very sight of them pollutes his exalted presence. Finally, foreigners, on the whole, have learned to respect our traditions, but if a foreigner, in his unenlightened ignorance, fails to bow he is to be pitied rather than punished. Decapitation in such circumstances would be most inappropriate.

Japan From End to End

Because of the redistribution of domains previously noted, it is probably the case that since 1605 you have been living in a different area of Japan from the province where your parents were brought up. To assist those who find their surroundings unfamiliar, I include here a guide to the regions and provinces of Japan, written as an imaginary journey. A helpful map (showing all the roads, battles towns and temples that I mention) has been included on pages 180–81.

Let us begin in the far north of our glorious empire. Here lies the island of Hokkaido, a wild, cold and unexplored land inhabited by fierce hairy men who sacrifice bears. One day they will be civilized. There is very little else to say about Hokkaido. It is exceedingly unpleasant so we will quickly move on. The northern part of Honshu, the main island of Japan, is called Tohoku. Until comparatively recently this land was almost as wild as Hokkaido. Now it is ruled on the shogun's behalf by noble pioneering families such as the Date, Nambu and Satake. There are many mountains here and the forests are full of bears. In winter the snow covers the roofs of houses. The province is most disagreeable, so we will hurry through it.

Moving further south we encounter the rich and fertile plain of the Kanto, a blessed land indeed. For centuries the provinces of the Kanto area have been the cradles of brave samurai, so it is only fitting that the greatest city in Japan is also located here. This is Edo, the capital city of His Most Excellent Highness the shogun, where the Tokugawa family have resided for many years. Edo is so much more important and so much more splendid than the emperor's capital of Kyoto (see below) that some have taken to calling Edo 'Tokyo' (eastern capital). This is an interesting idea but I don't think it will catch on.

'Kanto' of course means 'east of the barrier', and some of the Kanto provinces are indeed bounded on their southern or western sides by the natural barrier of huge mountains, which include the peerless and beautiful Mount Fuji. Lords chosen by his Most Excellent Highness carefully guard the passes that run through the mountains, ensuring peace within the realm.

Two great roads head westwards from Edo through these mountain passes. The first is a wild and difficult route called the Nakasendo, which makes its way through the mountainous province of Shinano. The other is the Tokaido Road, which follows the coastline and is infinitely more agreeable.

A samurai practising kyudo (archery) using the Japanese longbow. Archery is one of the most ancient of the martial arts.

On leaving Edo, the Tokaido Road passes first through the exquisite village of Kawasaki, a place whose name – thanks to the temple of Kobo Daishi – is synonymous with peace and tranquillity. After Kawasaki, the road wends its way past the ancient capital of Kamakura, goes over the wild Hakone Pass beneath Mount Fuji and then heads down towards Mikawa and Totomi, the provinces from where the Tokugawa family originated. Here is the town of Toyota, a place of skilled craftsmen.

The two great roads merge beside the shore of beautiful Lake Biwa and pass along the narrow neck of land that marks the centre of Japan, finishing their journey in Kyoto, the city that has been the capital of His Divine Majesty the emperor for 700 years. Many are the wonders to be seen in Kyoto, and the greatest of these are the exquisite gardens of the Zen temples, where subtle miniature landscapes enchant the eye. I have always enjoyed the gardens of Kyoto, but alas, one of the finest of all gardens is now ruined. Five years ago the six majestic cherry trees that filled the garden of the Ryoanji Temple succumbed to blight and had to be removed. All that is left now is a wide expanse of sand and fifteen rather dull rocks. It is most distressing.

South of Kyoto lies the mighty castle of Osaka, where misguided rebels still lurk. May they soon be crushed! Should you take ship westwards from Osaka you will find yourself on the Inland Sea, an agreeable area dotted with little islands where fierce pirates once lurked. The southern shores of the Inland Sea encompass the northern coast of the island of Shikoku, whose four provinces of Sanuki, Iyo, Awa and Tosa hold much of interest. Continuing westwards across the Inland Sea we come to the narrow Shimonoseki Strait that separates Honshu from the great southern Japanese island of Kyushu. How marvellous this island is – and yet how often a source of irritation! It was to the ports of Kyushu that the Southern Barbarians first came, bringing their guns and their evil religion. There are many great samurai families located in provinces in Kyushu whose names alone chill the blood. Who can utter 'Satsuma' without emotion?

Beyond Kyushu we find many tropical coral islands with waving palms and seas of the deepest blue. This paradise is Ryukyu, which some call Okinawa, the noble king of which pays tribute to the Chinese emperor and trades with his celestial empire. Having regard for the ancient lineage and independence of this noble kingdom, Japan will never interfere in its harmonious existence. Ryukyu shares the peace that our great empire now enjoys under the Tokugawa family.

Foreigners at a Glance

There are a great number of foreigners in Japan. You may well meet a foreigner during the course of your duties. Please do not be alarmed – most are perfectly harmless. The only offensive thing you are likely to note about them (particularly the English) is their unpleasant smell. All are merchants and traders, because priests and other religious persons were eliminated from Japan a few years ago. As previously noted, if you meet a foreigner you must not expect him to bow to you, but if he does then the slightest nod will suffice in return. There is no need to draw your sword.

The Chinese

There have been Chinese people living in Japan for thousands of years. They are industrious, hard-working and law-abiding. The Chinese are also very clever, particularly in military matters. Did you know that they invented gunpowder? (See 'Exploding Cows' in chapter 10.) Most of the Chinese you will meet call themselves merchants, which may be a little surprising to hear because all trade between China and Japan was banned by the Ming emperor several decades ago. You can trade with them with confidence, but insist on payment in cash and avoid using the word 'pirate'. It upsets them.

The Koreans

Relations with Korea have been a little strained since we invaded them in 1592, laid their country to waste and slaughtered thousands of their civilians. Have dealings with them by all means, but DON'T MENTION THE WAR.

The Portuguese and the Spanish

As a result of a shipwreck in 1543 the Portuguese became the first Europeans to arrive in Japan. They soon came to dominate the Chinese silk trade, and all would have been well had they not insisted on preaching the evil religion of Christianity. Thankfully reason has now prevailed; all their priests have been expelled and Christianity has almost completely disappeared. By and large the Portuguese traders who remain in Japan are comparatively civilized. They always bow, take baths willingly, never forget to remove their footwear on entering a house and always do their best to learn Japanese. They will, however, insist on eating meat, which is a waste of useful animals. They also drink wine made from grapes – an odd idea, but if you happen to be offered some, I hear that 1597 was a good year. As for the Spanish, they are very like the Portuguese, but unfortunately prone to conquering other nations, so we have to be on our guard against them.

The Dutch

The Dutch first came here in 1600. They are very different from the Portuguese, whom they dislike. Their version of Christianity is also said to be different, although no one in Japan can fathom out how this may be. Unlike the Portuguese, they do not favour taking baths. They wear coarse cloth instead of silk and therefore smell. They also eat a disgusting substance called 'cheese'.

The English

These foreigners cause more trouble than anyone else, even though there are very few of them. The English smell worse than the Dutch and are always starting fights. Although you are advised not to approach them (particularly when they are drunk) be assured that their intentions are largely honourable. One of them, a Captain William Adams, has found favour with His Most Illustrious Highness, whom he has advised on several matters. In fact, Englishmen can be very good company; it is also a point in their favour that, like the Dutch, they have no truck with the Spanish or the Portuguese on the question of religion. Indeed, when the Spanish tried to invade England in 1588 their fleet was wrecked by a kamikaze. It has been remarked by more than one observer that as a result of this religious enmity the English distrust the Spanish and Portuguese even more than we do.

2
From Samurai to Samurai Warrior

The Way of the Samurai is found in death.

NABESHIMA TSUNETOMO, *HIDDEN AMONG LEAVES*

Am I a Real Samurai? – Take Our Helpful Quiz

Having sketched out for you the nature and history of this warrior nation of ours, it is time to turn to the most important topic of all: the way that you become a true samurai warrior. I am sure you are eager to begin your study; but, even though you have been born into that most glorious of social classes, are you really samurai material? See how you score in this simple quiz:

1 'Samurai' literally means 'those who serve', so all samurai are:
a) *Servants*
b) *Lewd and sordid persons*
c) *Noble warriors*

2 An arquebus (matchlock musket) is fired by:
a) *Dropping a lighted match on to powder in the touchhole*
b) *Lewd and sordid persons*
c) *Both of the above*

3 The face mask on your suit of armour has a detachable nosepiece ornamented with whiskers. Its function is to:

a) *Provide a secure location for tying the helmet cords*
b) *Present a brave and terrifying appearance to your enemy*
c) *Show your superiority over lewd and sordid persons*

4 A yamabushi (wandering exorcist) pronounces a curse upon you. Should you:

a) *Curse him back*
b) *Worry that you have offended the gods and make a hurried reparation*
c) *Cut his head off*

5 You have discovered that your favourite concubine is a secret Christian. Should you:

a) *Ignore the matter and continue the relationship*
b) *Report her to the magistrate and have her investigated*
c) *Cut her head off*

6 A drunken Englishman insults you in the streets of Nagasaki. Should you:

a) *Ignore him and thank the gods you were born Japanese*
b) *Buy him a drink and have the best evening since you came back from the Korean War*
c) *Cut his head off*

7 You are leaving to go on campaign when your lord falls off his horse. Should you:

a) *Refuse to fight for such an inauspicious leader whom the gods clearly detest*
b) *March on regardless*
c) *Exclaim 'What good fortune. The gods of war are impatient for our inevitable victory!'*

8 You are performing the tea ceremony when one of your ladies-in-waiting breaks wind. Do you:

a) *Ignore the insult and continue, displaying an admirable Zen-like composure*

b) *Cut off her head and continue, displaying an admirable Zen-like composure*

c) *Continue, displaying an admirable Zen-like composure, and then cut off her head when you have finished*

9 You are awakened from your sleep by a terrifying nightmare in which you are accosted by the screaming skulls of all the samurai you have ever killed. Do you:

a) *Rejoice in their misfortune and your own good favour*

b) *Resolve to fight no more, shave your head and become a monk*

c) *Decide never to drink cheap sake again*

10 Your lord intends to send you on a dangerous mission into enemy territory from which you will probably never return. Do you:

a) *Refuse to go*

b) *Suggest alternatives*

c) *Accept without question*

How Did You Score?

9 – 10 Well done. You are exactly the sort of young person for whom this book is intended. Study it well.

6 – 8 Not bad, you have obviously got a lot to learn, but this is the book for you.

3 – 5 You may wish to reconsider a martial career. There is always a huge demand for reliable book-keepers in Edo, and as a member of the samurai class you will still be allowed to wear a sword.

Answers: 1–c, 2–c, 3–b, 4–c, 5–a, b or c, 6–a, 7–c, 8–c, 9–a, 10–c
(Information relating to the answers will be found later in the book.)

1 – 2 Are you sure you are not a lewd and sordid person? Please check your lineage.

0 You are obviously a foreigner, so read this book and tremble.

Bushido – The Soul of Japan

In the view of His Most Excellent Highness, no member of the samurai class can consider himself to be a true samurai warrior until he fully understands both his place and his role in society. The overall social hierarchy into which you fit was outlined in Chapter 1, and here I delineate the most important principles of behaviour that are applicable to samurai. Make sure that you study this section in great detail before moving on to the chapters about fighting, no matter how tempting that may be. The points outlined below are fundamental to samurai behaviour and will help set you above members of the lower classes, foreigners and other lewd and sordid persons.

The social duty incumbent upon a samurai is to share his virtue with those below him and to act as an example to them; nothing is more necessary than for him to provide a constant demonstration of filial piety. The samurai honours his lord just as the son honours his father, and this is the glue that binds our society together.

For society to be harmonious, of course, filial piety must extend throughout all the social classes. However, it is only the samurai class who practise the other great truth – the code of conduct known as bushido, which is both the Way of the Warrior and the soul of Japan. Now to some extent this book is entirely about bushido, for the code encompasses the totality of the samurai life, so I will say little about it at this stage except for providing a definition of and one outstanding example of it.

A Japanese samurai lord (daimyo), seated with his right arm on an arm rest.
For an ordinary samurai, his lord is the absolute focus of loyalty.

The key precept of loyalty to the point of death makes bushido the outward manifestation of filial piety, while in its commitment to a noble life it also provides a set of behaviours and expectations that readily distinguish a samurai from lewd and sordid persons. Besides being loyal, a samurai is also benevolent, honourable, brave, polite, self-controlled and unostentatious. Benevolence is the attitude he shows to the lower orders because he cares for their welfare as a father cares for his children. His honour is a jewel to be preserved, for without it his life would cease to have meaning. His bravery will be shown most readily on the battlefield, but there will be many times in ordinary life when courage is required. So too he must exhibit politeness, for courtesy is the stamp of greatness. To ensure that none of these virtues is wasted through pride or unnecessary self-aggrandizement, the samurai is also self-controlled and self-denying. Finally, his lack of attachment to worldly wealth is made plain to all through his modest dress and deportment – a virtue also demonstrated by his reluctance to indulge in overeating or drunkenness. 'The samurai has not eaten, but still picks his teeth', is a proverb that illustrates very well this aspect of self-control.

Let me give one outstanding example of bushido in action. It was in accordance with bushido that Torii Mototada sacrificed himself for

His Most Illustrious Highness at the siege of Fushimi Castle in 1600. Lord Torii was defending the castle against an army sent by His Most Illustrious Highness's enemies and had few options but surrender as the castle blazed around him. Yet he fought on to the bitter end, thus gaining time that allowed His Most Illustrious Highness to take a position from which he might vanquish his foes. Torii Mototada finally committed suicide as his castle fell. His loyal and unquestioning defence of the doomed castle was futile, but it had also kept many thousands of enemy samurai away from the battle of Sekigahara, at which His Most Illustrious Highness consequently triumphed. His loyalty was meritorious indeed.

In the pages that follow you will learn all you need to know about bushido. Honour it as you honour your ancestors, because it must never be forgotten that the duties of filial piety extend beyond the grave: you must honour your ancestors as you would your own living father. It is their meritorious deeds that have provided the example of bushido that you now follow. How blessed is the samurai of whom it can be said 'By his conduct he has honoured his ancestors.' Yet how much more blessed is that rare individual of whom it can be said 'He has exceeded his ancestors in glory and martial virtue.' Let it be you of whom this is recorded.

Frequently Asked Questions About Loyalty and Revenge

Q My lord has died. Should I commit suicide and join him as a guest in the White Jade Pavilion?

A No, the loyalty that you gave to him in life is now automatically transferred to his heir, who will need your continued service. This is such an important principle that the practice of following one's lord in death is strictly forbidden in law as well as in custom.

Q My lord has ordered me to be adopted into a family that has no heir. I am distressed at the prospect of leaving the family I have always known and changing my name. What should I do?

A You must accept without question. Exactly this situation happened to me, and, although I am now known by a different name, I know that my cousins who remain in the Honda family will never desert me.

Q My lord has been murdered. What should I do now?

A You must avenge him. The duty of revenge is absolutely fundamental. As the old Chinese proverb says, 'No son can live under the same heaven as the murderer of his father.' Through the doctrine of filial piety you are your lord's son. His murderer must be sought out and killed. It is, however, important to note that there are rules about how this may be done. His Most Excellent Highness is at pains to distinguish between a legitimate vendetta and disorderly killing outside the rule of law. It has therefore been decreed that any man seeking to avenge another must first give notice of his intent to the local machi bugyo (magistrate). If this means that the intended victim is forewarned of the avenger's intentions, then so be it. For avengers to launch a surprise attack on their unsuspecting victim would be to disgrace the name of the samurai for evermore. However, I am sure this rule could be disregarded if the vengeance is carried out in the heat of the moment, so if you have to take revenge, do it speedily, and may the gods be with you.

Q My lord has joined our enemies. Should I follow him?

A This is a very difficult question to answer because you owe loyalty to your lord, yet in changing sides he has been disloyal to his own lord. What is the faithful samurai to do? My general answer would be that a loyal samurai should counsel his master as to the consequences likely to arise from taking such a drastic step, although I believe this question can really be answered on only a case-by-case basis. Take Akechi Mitsuhide, who was marching his army to the west in 1582 and then suddenly ordered them to turn round and attack the residence of Lord Oda Nobunaga, who was most grievously killed. The samurai obeyed Lord Akechi, but then went to their doom when he was in turn vanquished by Toyotomi Hideyoshi, who avenged his dead master at the battle of Yamazaki. Those samurai should instead have tried to dissuade Akechi from taking such a dreadful course of action, and if he persisted in it, they should not have followed him but should all have committed suicide in protest, for that is the Way of the Warrior.

Q My lord's heir is to be married to a lady from a family whose pedigree is questionable. Should I speak out?

A Indeed you should, but first make sure that you have all the necessary facts to hand. Your lord will appreciate your diligence in this most sensitive of areas. If at all possible, obtain a copy of the lady's pedigree, and do not be afraid to challenge it. Is she claiming descent from ancestors who did not actually exist? Do any of the names that appear there sound unusual when read aloud? If so, she could be Korean.

Q My lord is sending me to certain death. What should I do?

A Go to certain death.

Nine Samurai Whom it Would Be Auspicious to Emulate

We can all learn from the past, so before we leave the general question of samurai behaviour let us consider nine individuals whom I have chosen to illustrate the above points. The loyalty and other martial virtues displayed by these men set the standard for others to follow. You will note (to your certain surprise) that the following list does not include the names of His Most Illustrious Highness the Retired Shogun or His Most Excellent Highness the Shogun. This is because both men surpass all others in martial virtue and excellence, and so none can emulate them.

Minamoto Yoshiie (1041–1108)

Minamoto Yoshiie, ancestor of the first shogun, was unsurpassed in military virtue and a master of the Way of Horse and Bow. So valiant was Yoshiie that he earned the nickname 'First-born Son of Hachiman'. To be compared to a son of the god of war – what an honour that was! He was also noted for the care he took over the welfare of his followers, who suffered greatly during the harsh winters in Tohoku. In this manner did Yoshiie exercise the virtue of benevolence. Take heed of it.

Minamoto Yoshitsune (1159–89)

Yoshitsune was the younger brother of the first shogun, Minamoto Yoritomo, and won three great victories during the Gempei War. At Ichinotani in 1184 he conducted a surprise attack on the rear of the Ichinotani Fortress by leading his horsemen down a steep cliff. At Yashima he again triumphed over the Taira, only for them to escape to their boats. In the following year of 1185 he completely vanquished them at the most memorable battle of Dan no Ura, when the sea ran red with the blood of the slain. You should admire Yoshitsune for his martial virtue and for the loyalty he showed to his brother.

Hojo Tokimune (1251–84)

Is it possible to be a great leader of samurai without ever lifting your sword in anger? Indeed it is, and Hojo Tokimune provides the example. He was the ruler of Japan when the Mongols attacked, and it was his inspired leadership that persuaded the samurai of Japan to fight to their deaths against the foreign invaders. Tokimune was also devoted to the worship of the Buddha according to the Zen school and followed the path of self-denial that it requires. Take heed of this, for it is part of the Way of the Warrior.

Hojo Soun, the first of the five generations of Hojo lords who ruled much of the Kanto from their castle at Odawara until being defeated by Toyotomi Hideyoshi in 1590.

Kusunoki Masashige (1294–1336)

There can be no better example of the virtue of loyalty than Kusunoki Masashige, who fought for the emperor against the Hojo family who had usurped the shogunate. He is best known for his death at the battle of Minatogawa in 1336. Masashige knew that the emperor's cause was hopeless, but he obeyed the imperial command and died fighting. Let this manifestation of the Way of the Warrior followed to the point of certain death be an example to us all.

Ashikaga Yoshimitsu (1358–1408)

The Ashikaga branch of the Minamoto family supplied 15 shoguns, and none was more accomplished than Yoshimitsu: it is to him that we owe the reconciliation between the rival courts and the restoration of peace to Japan. He was also a skilled general who in 1400 defeated Ouchi Yoshihiro, a man who unwisely tried to seize the position of shogun. When peace had been restored, Yoshimitsu showed his true greatness by re-establishing the friendship with China (relations had been soured by the Mongol invasions) and building the Golden Pavilion that now graces the landscape northwest of Kyoto. Truly he was accomplished both in the arts of war and the arts of peace.

Hojo Soun (1432–1519)

Some people condemn Hojo Soun for being an upstart, and it is true that he was of humble origins and began his samurai career with only six followers. Yet the gods smiled on him and blessed him with victory, so one may forgive him even for taking the name of Hojo, which was not his originally. For four generations, each successive son admirably followed the doctrine of filial piety, and Soun provided them with as noble an ancestor as any samurai could hope for. They ruled the Kanto provinces until eventually humbled by the martial skill of His Most Illustrious Highness.

Uesugi Kenshin (1530–78)

People sometimes ask me 'Who was the greater of the two rivals Uesugi Kenshin and Takeda Shingen?' and I always answer 'Kenshin'. Why? Because even though nearly every contest between the two of them (they fought five battles at a place called Kawanakajima) was indecisive, the same cannot be said about the wars they fought against others. At Mikata ga Hara, Shingen came close to defeating His Most Illustrious Highness, and would have done so had it not been for the all-encompassing military virtue that His Most Illustrious Highness displayed during the ordered withdrawal. However, at Tedorigawa Uesugi, Kenshin defeated Oda Nobunaga – the only person ever to do such a thing.

Oda Nobunaga (1534–82)

In the sad days when His Most Illustrious Highness was a young man and a vassal of the ill-fated Imagawa family, he took part in a campaign against Lord Oda Nobunaga, covering himself in martial glory (even though the Imagawa ultimately failed). Nobunaga was a wise leader and recognized the talent of His Most Illustrious Highness, who soon became his ally. Lord Oda then went from strength to strength, defeating myriad enemies. Only one of his generals failed to be loyal to him. This was the despicable Akechi Mitsuhide, who had Nobunaga murdered. After this appalling act Lord Akechi lived for just 13 days before being killed in battle. Let it be a lesson to us all.

Toyotomi Hideyoshi (1536–98)

How can I fail to include the man who unified Japan? His greatness as a general and as a statesman was unsurpassed in the age, and, after all, he even defeated His Most Illustrious Highness at Nagakute in 1584. Hideyoshi's victories at Yamazaki and Shizugatake were masterly indeed, and he then went on to conquer the islands of Shikoku and Kyushu – even challenging the might of the Ming empire. Note also how loyal his generals were to him, even going willingly to certain death. True loyalty ideally follows fine leadership, and Toyotomi Hideyoshi was a samurai's general.

Female Samurai Warriors – How Should You React?

You may be surprised by the inclusion of this section, but I feel that it is necessary, because in 1590 a rather embarrassing incident occurred during the siege of Hondo Castle on the Amakusa Islands in Higo province. The castle was being defended by deceitful Christian rebels, who had been seduced by foreign priests into taking up arms against their rightful lord. As a result of this obnoxious behaviour, Kato Kiyomasa, Lord of Kumamoto, marched against them and began a siege. While the operation was in progress, the gates of Hondo Castle unexpectedly opened to disgorge 300 women who charged wildly at Lord Kato's samurai, swinging their curve-bladed spears. Many of his samurai were killed, and this was largely due – I believe – to their reluctance to engage the women in battle. This unfortunate lapse lasted only a few minutes, but was sufficiently serious to bring about the deaths of several noble samurai (the mode of whose passing, it must be admitted, was far from meritorious).

It must be emphasized that fighting women are an extremely rare phenomenon. In the case of Hondo they also fell into the category of lewd and sordid persons who had failed to appreciate the inherent martial virtues of the samurai class. That the women at Hondo were Christians only adds to the enormity of their despicable behaviour.

To set against this bad example, there are also several praiseworthy instances when the wives of lords (their husbands being absent when their castles were unexpectedly attacked by enemies) took it upon themselves to organize the defence. For example, at exactly the same time that Lord Torii was defending Fushimi on behalf of His Most Illustrious Highness, Anotsu Castle in Ise province also came under attack. Its commander, Tomita Nobutaka, was away serving in the army of His Most Illustrious Highness, so the defence was most valiantly undertaken in his absence by his wife Yuki-no-kata. Similarly, far away on the Nakasendo Road, Lord Sanada Nobuyuki was forced to leave his wife in charge of Numata Castle. So forceful was her refusal to surrender the castle to their enemies that the siege was abandoned.

These are extreme examples, but your sister belongs to the samurai class too; she must of course learn the budo (martial arts) that are suitable for the fairer sex in case her honour is ever challenged. She will then be able either to defend herself to the death or to commit suicide (in order to avoid bringing dishonour upon the family). Furthermore, as the above examples demonstrate, you never know what other challenges might appear and how she might react. Never underestimate a woman.

3
Armour, Swords and Costumes to Adorn the Warrior

When he goes forth to war the soldier is prepared for the assault of arrow and gunshot, ready to leap into fire and boiling water. His dauntless behaviour may be due to his loyal spirit and natural courage, but if his armour be not strong he can avail but little.

HAYAKAWA KYUKEI, FROM THE PREFACE TO
THE MANUFACTURE OF ARMOUR AND HELMETS

From the tip of his pigtail to the soles of his sandals the samurai warrior is indeed an impressive sight, but there is no chance element in this, because in his selection of weapons and costume the samurai is guided and garbed by tradition.

Samurai Swords – Handle With Care

Among his many weapons, none is more important to a warrior than the one that will be closest to him for the rest of his life – his samurai sword. No weapon in the entire world excels it. It is said that a good sword can do two remarkable things. First, when held in a stream with the blade facing the running current, it will sever a lotus flower floated downstream the moment that the bloom touches the cutting edge of the sword. Second, it will cut through seven corpses piled on top of each other above a bed of sand. I have heard tell of one noble samurai who

45

was offended by a peasant, and struck him with his sword so sharply and with a blow so fierce that he cut the man cleanly from his neck to his groin. Yet so rapidly and keenly was the blow delivered that the man walked on for six paces before falling in two.

Whatever his prowess in other martial arts, a samurai is known by his skills with the famous samurai sword. Made by craftsmen and hallowed by tradition, it is the finest cutting weapon in the entire world.

Your sword will have been created by a master craftsman, who, should society ever permit it, must surely deserve the title of samurai in spite of his apparently vulgar position. Such men are characteristically modest, referring to themselves as blacksmiths rather than sword-makers or swordsmiths. Beginning with iron-sand taken from the riverbeds of Japan, these miracle workers, dressed in white robes that would befit a priest, first create iron itself, which is then heated, beaten and reheated to make steel. They then take this unshaped steel and beat it, bend it and beat it again, all the while stretching the metal into a shape that begins to resemble the final blade.

The finished sword consists of a number of different parts, all of which fit together to make a complete whole, just as is the case with the samurai – for as we all have our own role to play in the order of things, so we are very like parts of sword. The blade fits into a wooden handle that is covered with the skin of the giant ray and bound with cord to give a secure grip. It slips into a scabbard, on either side of which are kept concealed two sharp knives. The sword takes no chances. Good samurai are like that.

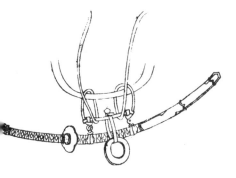

Throughout history the badge of the samurai has been his sword. In this picture we see the sword tied around the waist in tachi style, rather than in katana style with the sword thrust through the belt, cutting side uppermost.

What the Well-Dressed Samurai is Wearing

When not actually wearing armour, you will still be magnificently attired in a costume that varies little from one lord to another except in the colour of the cloth and the family crest that is sewn on to it. Over the top of your long kimono you will wear wide trousers called hakama, into which are tucked the ends of your kataginu, a small, winged jacket with stiffened shoulders. This elegant combination is called a kami-shimo. When riding or marching you will replace your hakama with tighter trousers, and wear a loose haori jacket instead of the kataginu.

Ceremonial Clothes and How Not to Fall Over in Them

Problems may arise when you are received in audience at the court of His Most Excellent Highness, for there you will be required to wear nagabakama, which represent the greatest sartorial trap for the unprepared samurai. As you will guess from the name, these are long trousers (very long trousers!), indeed the legs extend right over your feet. The idea is, I am assured by those closer to His Most Excellent Highness, that no one wearing nagabakama could carry out an assassination. This is a conclusion with which I am broadly in agreement. In fact someone wearing nagabakama can hardly move at all, except by dragging each leg behind him in turn like two enormous elephants' trunks. At least His Most Excellent Highness is safe from being murdered, which is the most important thing. As far as you are concerned, when attending an audience at court (which is a nerve-wracking ordeal at the best of times) the last thing you should have to worry about is falling over your own trousers. Make sure you obtain a pair at least a month beforehand and practise in the privacy of your own home. It can be done – just take it *very* gently.

Your Hair and When You Should Let it Down

Foreigners often remark on the care a samurai takes over his hair. It is customary, as you know, to shave off the front portion of one's hair and tie the remainder back in a doubled-over pigtail. Alternatively it is quite acceptable to leave all the hair intact and tie it back in a single pigtail, rather like a tea whisk. One's hair should always look immaculate, and the field of battle is the only time when you can let your hair down.

Needless to say, preparation is as essential on the field of war as it is on any occasion. One's hair is not merely allowed to lie casually beneath one's helmet. You must remove the cords binding the pigtail, comb the hair straight and then tie a white headband across your forehead. The white colour signals your determination to die. Your hair will naturally become dishevelled when you are fighting, but don't worry, because some young lady will be given the job of making sure that your hair is neat and tidy after your head has been cut off. It will then be presented to the enemy general, and you will look very proud.

To add the finishing touch to the excellence of your coiffure, why not burn a little incense inside your helmet before putting it on? That way, when your head is cut off, your hair will bear a pleasant odour and people will be sure to remark on your good taste.

Japanese Armour and Why It is Superior to All Others

Some samurai have been known to gaze upon a suit of European armour, such as the one once presented to His Most Illustrious Highness by the Portuguese viceroy of the Indies, and exclaim 'I'd like one like that.' How misguided they are! Only a coward would wish to be encased from head to foot in steel, with just narrow slits for his eyes. Who would ever want to see arrows bouncing off his suit of armour when they could remain embedded in it to show the warrior's bravery? Besides, who would want to wear a suit of armour in which the only way to commit ritual disembowelment would be to stick a dagger up his unhinged codpiece? How ridiculous! No, for the valiant samurai the Japanese suit of armour is without peer.

The first pieces of armour to be put on over the armour robe are the suneate. They consist of a series of iron plates sewn on to a cloth backing.

- - - - - - - - - -

Why should this be? Well, a Japanese suit of armour is constructed in a very different way from European armours. Ours are not made from large steel plates, but are instead referred to as being 'lamellar', which means that they consist of a large number of small metal plates that are lacquered and then tied together, thus making a suit of Japanese armour a highly complex object. Let us examine one from the inside out by imagining a samurai getting dressed for battle.

Putting on Your Armour

The first things you will have put on will be your loincloth and your shirt. Above the shirt you will wear an armour robe. This is like an ordinary kimono but much simpler in design. A pair of trousers go on top of that. The ensemble is then secured using a belt, and gaiters are tied round the calves. Now refer to the accompanying illustrations, because along

The armoured haidate, protection for the thigh area, is fastened around the waist.

- - - - - - -

The kote consists of a pair of cloth sleeves to which plates and chain mail are attached at vulnerable points. Sometimes, as in this case, the sleeves are made as one.

-- -- -- -- -- -- -- -- -- --

The largest section of a samurai's armour consists of the do, to which the kusazuri are attached. The do is usually hinged at one side and tied using shoulder-straps that also take its weight. It is secured at the waist using a belt.

-- -- -- -- -- -- -- -- -- -- -- -- --

The sode are a pair of shoulder-protectors made like small composite armour plates. They are suspended from the shoulder-straps of the do.

-- -- -- -- -- -- -- -- -- -- -- --

The mempo (face mask) is one of the most characteristic features of a Japanese suit of armour. Although originally intended simply as a safe anchorage for the cords of the helmet, it has become customary to decorate the face mask with moustaches and teeth to intimidate enemy warriors during battle.

-- -- -- -- -- --

come the first pieces of armour, which are the suneate (shin-guards) that will also protect your calves. The samurai then puts on his haidate (thigh-guards), an article that looks rather like an armoured apron. Two kote (sleeves) will protect your arms, and on top of these is worn the do (body armour), from which are suspended the kusazuri (tassets), rather like little armoured skirts. Two sode (shoulder-guards) will be attached to the outside of the shoulder straps of the do, while round your waist will be tied your sword-belt.

Your face and throat will be protected by a shikoro (neck-guard) and a face mask, and it is the fashion nowadays to ornament the mask with horse-hair moustaches and silver teeth. The original idea of the face mask was to provide a secure surface for tying the helmet cords, but its further utility in war was soon appreciated: when your enemy sees you approaching he may well flee in terror from the devilish being that you have become.

Choosing the Correct Helmet

The final illustration in the accompanying set of pictures shows a simple battledress helmet, which is really all you need to protect your skull, although you may be tempted to embellish your suit of armour by buying a magnificent design. Here I must sound a note of caution. If you are a general then it is fine to wear a helmet that sports gigantic buffalo horns, peacock-tail plumes or Chinese sword-blades, or even to choose a helmet shaped like the head of a monkey. What is frequently forgotten is that generals have helmet-bearers to carry their headgear for them, because these elaborate items are donned only when the battle is over and the general has the leisure and the security to indulge in post-battle rituals, such as head viewing. At other times the helmet bearer, who stands next to the general, carries the helmet on a spear-shaft. In short, these helmets are not suitable for combat. Besides, simply to wear a general's style of helmet will cause resentment among your comrades, who will accuse you of ostentation, which is not in accordance with the Way of the Warrior.

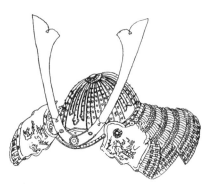

The final item of samurai armour is the vital kabuto (helmet). Generals wear very elaborate helmets, but a simple and sturdy battledress helmet is best for fighting in.

- - - - - - - - - - - - - - -

This is an example of the old style of helmet, made for the type of armour known as a yoroi. Note the wide neck-guard and the decorative kuwagata (antlers). These splendid objects are still worn centuries later by high-ranking samurai.

- - - - - - - - - - - - - - - -

Accessories – The Finishing Touch

Many are the accessories available to go with your chosen suit of armour. Some are fairly obvious, such as a water bottle, spare sandals, a medicine kit and a bag for carrying severed heads in, but don't clutter up your person with unnecessary items – what do you think servants are for? Lastly, please don't neglect your horse. Suits of armour are now available for horses in a wide range of styles and fittings. Many consist of jackets of plate and cloth, some with very appealing chamfrons that will make your horse look like a dragon.

What Not to Wear

I know this will annoy some people, but I have to say something about embossed armour. Yes, to have a phoenix engraved upon your breast-plate and picked out in gold lacquer looks nice; but it weakens the armour. Ask yourself, what do you really want: something that looks fancy or something that is guaranteed to stop a bullet? I know which I would choose! Also, please try to avoid a suit of armour that is basically a mongrel. If the design of the breastplate and the sleeves don't match up, then the discrepancy will quickly be noticed. Try to have a suit of armour made that has your family crest lacquered on every plate, then you will not be tempted to pick and mix. Oh, and another thing, heavy shin-guards and bearskin boots – no! They are just SO Kamakura period.

4
The Martial Arts – Just How Good Are You?

The sword is the soul of the samurai.

TOKUGAWA IEYASU, *PRECEPTS*

✛ ✛ ✛

Of all samurai abilities, none is more important than prowess at the martial arts: it is through them that you become a true samurai. The first shogun, Minamoto Yoritomo, was a great statesman, but he was foremost a superb martial artist. Without that accomplishment he would have earned no respect from his fellow samurai, nor indeed would he have been able to exercise his statesmanship if he had not already vanquished those whom he now ruled. Whatever rank one holds in the grand scheme of things, a superlative sword and a well-made suit of armour will be of use to their owner only if he has been trained in the martial arts.

Practise the Martial Arts: No Pain – No Gain

Wherever you live, your lord will probably employ a teacher of sword-fighting (or other martial arts) who has a distinguished record and has earned the honoured title of sensei – which means so much more than just 'teacher'. Over the years you will develop a close relationship with your sensei, and hopefully the skills of the great teacher will rub off on you. This man will be a superb martial arts practitioner in his own right and will hold a glorious position in your lord's army when he takes to the battlefield, but the greatest service he will render in his entire career is the training he provides for young samurai like you. He will certainly have in mind a training plan that will include kenjutsu and yarijutsu (sword- and spear-fighting techniques), as well as the use of specialized edged weapons such as the naginata (glaive), the dagger (tanto) and the nodachi (extra-long sword). Other specialists employed in your lord's entourage will cover archery, horsemanship and the vulgar, though sadly unavoidable, skills of gunnery and shooting.

The perennial problem for these experts lies in how to train young men like you in the use of real, sharp-edged weapons without thereby causing dreadful injuries. Well, one way is through the use of kata, which are set moves performed time and time again to rehearse every possible combination of thrust and counter-thrust. As the essence of kata lies in the fact that no contact is made, sword kata can be performed using real swords and spear kata with real spears. A very advanced form of training involves tsumeru, which is the use of real swords but with the blow pulled short of its target. Needless to say, this is very difficult to achieve, and no greater praise can be heaped upon a swordsman than to record of him that he has the skills and the control to perform tsumeru. The great swordsman Miyamoto Musashi (whom you may even meet one day as he makes one of his famous warrior pilgrimages round Japan, challenging worthy opponents) is supposed to be able to sever a grain of cooked rice placed upon an opponent's nose without breaking the man's skin.

When it comes to developing a samurai's skills with edged weapons, there is no substitute for hours and hours of practice using wooden imitations of the real thing. Some people think that using carved timber swords or spears is a soft option, but those people

The age-old problem of how to practise effectively with real swords has partly been solved by the introduction of the bokken. This is a wooden sword of the same weight as a steel sword, meaning realistic blows can be delivered.

- - - - - - - - - - - - - - - -

have never been knocked almost unconscious by a blow from a dummy weapon. For example, the bokken (wooden sword) is made from just oak, but it has the weight and the balance of a real sword, and can really hurt. The only thing it lacks is a keen metal edge, so be prepared to take the blows and give some back.

Real fights with real swords will occur on the battlefield, and there is no substitute for this experience; I must, however, make it clear that no lord should ever allow his young samurai to go out on to the highways and start fights just to practise their skills. That is not in accordance with the Way of the Warrior. One day, perhaps, just perhaps, you may become such a superlative swordsman that it will be fitting for you to venture on a warrior pilgrimage like those undertaken by Miyamoto Musashi, but you will do well to remember that not all of his dojo yaburi (challenges) are to the death. Musashi is not a murderer and does not consider it beneath his dignity to fight with a wooden sword if that is sufficient to convince a challenger of his superiority. Of course, if that challenger is not convinced that he has lost and insists on a fight with real swords then that is an entirely different matter. He may well end up being killed, and serve him right; the mere sight of Miyamoto Musashi drawing his sword is enough to persuade most opponents to surrender. All this is in accordance with the Way of the Warrior because, in the eloquent words of His Most Illustrious Highness, a sword is in its position of greatest strength when it lies sleeping in its scabbard.

A samurai swordsman holding his katana with one hand. His secondary weapon, the wakizashi (short-sword), is also thrust through his belt.

Sword-Fighting Techniques

A later section will describe how the sword is used to its best advantage on the battlefield, but in the dojo (practice hall) you will learn a series of techniques that are of universal application, whether you are fighting a friendly contest with wooden swords, or engaged in a duel to the death with steel blades.

The first principle you must understand is that, as well as being an attacking weapon, your sword provides you with defence. In many foreign countries warriors use things called shields, which are small boards carried in the non-striking hand that are used to receive an opponent's blow. The warrior then retaliates with a cut of his own delivered by the other hand. By contrast, Japanese swords are two-handed weapons, and if used properly can become their own shields, deflecting blows aimed against you as well as providing a means of following-up. A one-handed sword used in Europe called a rapier involves a similar idea, but the rapier is only a thrusting weapon. The Japanese sword can be used for both cutting (kiri) and thrusting (tsuki), and therein lies its unique qualities and strengths. When you practise sword-fighting, you will be taught to direct cutting attacks against the top of the head, the wrist, the side and the leg below the knee, with a thrusting movement being used to attack the throat. In a melee on the battlefield you will probably have to hit out at any target that presents itself, but these simple principles of attack are valuable because they strike at the most vulnerable parts of an unarmoured body.

Yet a list of preferred targets is much less important than the swordsman's overall attitude and composure. The self-control to appreciate a possible weak point and to deduce the means to attack it (perhaps even using an unorthodox sword-stroke), may well be the samurai's key to survival. The swordsman going into a contest must be completely calm. He will present an air of relaxation and detachment, even though he is totally alert and ready to spring out of the illusion of carelessness into sudden and violent action. He might therefore begin the contest with an iai stroke – a blow delivered straight from the scabbard. The sword is normally thrust through the belt with its cutting edge uppermost so that such a devastating initial blow may even win the contest in a single stroke. This is not the case with samurai in armour, who usually deliver the first blow using a spear, and so sling the sword from their belt.

SEIGAN
This is the classic fighting stance. The point of the blade is held towards the opponent's throat.

- - - - - - - - - - - - -

TAKANAMI
The sword is raised and held horizontally, as if preparing for a thrust.

- - - - - -

UKAGE KENNOSEI
This position looks almost casual, as if inviting your opponent to strike first.

- - - - - - - - -

We may envisage two swordsmen facing each other, their swords already drawn and their sword-tips almost touching. Many are the preferred stances adopted by renowned swordsmen: some will stand with the sword pointing forwards and its tip inclined slightly upwards (the seigan position); others will hold it almost vertical; and some keep it close to their faces with the cutting edge projecting forwards (the takanami position). Others have it held behind them in a seemingly careless manner, taunting their opponent to strike first – here the deadly stroke could well be the second blow that is delivered, the recipient having either dodged or deflected the first. In ordinary clothes a sword-cut against an unprotected arm or leg could well disable the victim, making no further blows necessary. In armour the situation is very different, and numerous blows will be exchanged before the combat is resolved.

DOFAN SO SEI
Two swordsmen in seigan stances clash their swords in cutting strokes.

NUSHIN JUKENNOSEI
The swordsman in takanami has his sword blocked by his opponent's upward sweep.

INSHIN NO KIRIME
A sudden undeflected thrust by the swordsman on the left takes his blade towards his opponent's heart.

- - - - - - - - - -   - - - - - - - - -   - - - - - - - - - - - -

The ferocity of a sword-cut must always be complemented by the swordsman's delicacy of movement. He should be able to slide and glide in smooth, controlled turns that are executed as gracefully as a shrine maiden performing a dance for the gods. By these means a cut delivered against him may simply be sidestepped rather than parried, leaving his opponent in a very vulnerable position. Various ryu (schools of sword-fighting) have their own favourite sets of movements, just as they have their own preferred techniques of cutting and thrusting. One sensei may speak of his 'dragonfly technique', another of his favourite 'light-ning strike', both of which will be complete mysteries to those who are not his pupils.

KAISIN NO KIRIME
Stepping smoothly to the side, the swordsman on the left avoids his opponent's cut, responding with a slash of his own.

JUSHIN NO KIRIME
A slide to the right allows the swordsman to deliver a blow against his opponent's exposed wrists.

- - - - - - - - - - - - -   - - - - - - - - - - -

To illustrate the above points I will recount an incident related to me about Miyamoto Musashi, who was once simultaneously attacked by seven men. The ruffians made a circle around him, but Musashi stood quietly, putting them off guard with his remarkable composure. Then he suddenly exploded into action, drawing his sword in an iai stroke with his left hand and plunging it almost by instinct into the opponent standing behind him. Withdrawing the blade he switched it to his right hand and took out two more opponents with a swift horizontal slice, cutting down a fourth with the return sweep of the blade. The remaining three were now disorientated, and their initial advantage of numbers had been reduced. Wielding his sword in a kisagake (whip-like) slash, Musashi completed his victory.

Spears and Other Polearms

These remarks about swordplay are equally applicable to the training of samurai in the use of spears as well as other edged weapons. Indeed, I would go so far as to say that training for spear-fighting is more important than training for sword-fighting. Why? Simply because the spear will be your primary weapon on the battlefield, and it is only when you close with your enemy that you will draw your sword. So honour the Japanese sword of course, but if your spear-fighting techniques are not up to scratch you will not live long enough to use it.

The most important battlefield weapon for a samurai is the yari (straight spear). This is essentially a thrusting weapon that can be used on foot or from horseback.

The essence of successful spear-fighting lies in appreciating that the spear is primarily a thrusting weapon rather than a cutting weapon, and this piercing action may be performed either from horseback or on foot. The naginata (glaive) is quite different, because this is a cutting weapon mounted on a spear-shaft, and only the most expert practitioner can use one effectively from horseback. Superlative riding skills are also needed to wield the naginata, because you will have to control your horse using only your legs, so as to free up both arms for the weapon. The nodachi (field sword) is even more difficult to use from horseback as it is heavy and requires more agility. The amazing performance by the Makara (father and son) at the battle of Anegawa in 1570 is the only example I can think of where a nodachi was used by a mounted warrior. Furthermore, please do not be fooled by the giant nodachi you see in temples: these exaggerated weapons are made as offerings to the gods and are not intended for battlefield use.

Wielding the naginata (glaive) requires greater skill than the yari (spear) because of its curved blade. It is difficult to use from horseback, but the momentum given to the cutting edge by swinging the long shaft makes it a deadly weapon in the right hands.

The naginata has a long curved blade, and is used for fierce slashing strokes.

The Way of Horse and Bow

Many young warriors forget that centuries ago a samurai's worth was measured not by his skills at sword-fighting or spear-fighting, but by his prowess with a bow and arrow from the back of a horse. You were a good samurai if you could shoot an arrow into an enemy while galloping along on a horse – proficient in what was called the Way of Horse and Bow (the forerunner of the all-encompassing code to samurai behaviour that we now call the Way of the Warrior). Speaking as one who can neither ride nor shoot arrows well, I have the greatest respect for anyone who can do both at once; it is always a delight at certain shrine festivals to watch skilled young samurai dressed as huntsmen performing the martial art of yabusame. Yabusame involves galloping along a track and releasing three arrows in succession against fixed wooden targets. Alas, modern warfare, with its emphasis on meticulous movement and the control of large blocks of troops, is not what it used to be, making the opportunity for individual horse archery a rare thing indeed. Samurai nowadays are far more likely to be seen delivering a cavalry charge armed with spears or naginata. It is no less honourable, but it just isn't the same.

Equestrian skills are absolutely vital for a samurai, who has not only to ride a horse, but also to use weapons from the horse's back. The martial art of yabusame and hunting are both good training for a horseman.

Mounted archery, naturally, involves outstanding ability in the skills of both horsemanship and bowmanship, so how may these be practised? My answer is that from time immemorial no pursuit has surpassed hunting as a form of training for samurai. It still serves this function, even though it is now more frequently enjoyed simply for the thrill of the chase. Sadly, the techniques of hunting (along with those of warfare) have changed with the times. Animals are now driven by beaters into a wide corral where samurai spear them from their horses, bring them down with arrows or even (dare I mention it?) shoot them dead with guns. No, if hunting is to be a meaningful form of training you must ride out, seek your game and then pursue it across the landscape.

Hunting has long been regarded as good practice for mounted warfare, although now, in the Edo period, it's not what it used to be. The present custom is for game to be corralled by beaters rather than being pursued.

The Pistol – A Promising Innovation

My negative views on firearms are well known, but before we leave the question of horseback warfare I am delighted to be able to inform you that a new type of gunpowder weapon has recently been introduced. I think that it might transform mounted warfare, making it resemble once more the individual combat with bows at which your ancestors excelled. The new weapon is called a 'pistol', and from my own limited knowledge of it I believe that this may be what we have all been waiting for, because it enables a samurai to use a firearm without any connotations of vulgarity. A pistol is like a very short arquebus that you can hold steadily in one hand rather than two, making it ideal for the noble mounted samurai, as distinct from the ignoble unmounted foot soldier. What is most interesting about the pistol is that the powder in the chamber is ignited not by a slow match, with all that procedure's inherent dangers, but by a flint from which sparks emerge when a metal wheel rotates against it. It takes time to reload a pistol, of course, but as every noble samurai has attendants waiting upon him, this would be an ideal task for them to perform: while you fire two pistols your servant can be reloading a third. His Most Excellent Highness firmly believes that a pistol can be fired from the saddle with no loss of dignity, so at last we have a firearm that can be considered honourable for samurai to use in this often-depressing world of modern warfare.

The recently introduced wheel-lock pistol provides new opportunities for a Tokugawa-era samurai to join combat from horseback. Several pistols are employed, all of which are reloaded by servants.

Unarmed Combat – The Samurai's Last Resort

There may come a time on the battlefield when you have lost your spear, your sword and your dagger. In such circumstances bare hands will decide the outcome of combat, and a wide range of grappling arts exist to help you overcome your opponent. You may well have tried sumo wrestling, either for pleasure, training or as an offering to the gods, but even though sumo is very entertaining, there are other grappling techniques that will be of much greater use to you. The first is karate, which teaches you to use your fists and your feet as if they were sword-blades or spear-points. The second is ju-jutsu, a technique that enables you to throw an opponent, hold him down and apply subtle locks to his joints to immobilize him. The great advantage of learning ju-jutsu is that you may practise using full contact without the inherent risks associated with sword-play. So neglect ju-jutsu at your peril, and take heart from the example of Lord Kato Kiyomasa, who became one of the 'Seven Spears' (the day's most valiant warriors) at the battle of Shizugatake in 1583. He defeated his final opponent in a ju-jutsu contest that ended with both of them falling over a cliff.

Sumo wrestling is an ancient grappling art much performed at festivals. It is of limited use to a samurai, for whom ju-jutsu techniques are more suitable.

Unarmed combat is the samurai's last resort, and there exist a number of techniques in ju-jutsu whereby the unarmed fighter may overcome an opponent, such as throwing him on to his back or placing force against his joints to immobilize him.

How to Swim in a Suit of Armour

When you read the old chronicles and battle stories that I recommend in a later section, you will be struck by the number of times skilled samurai swam their horses across rivers so that they might be first into battle. Certain of your contemporaries, however, go even further than that. Many years ago I visited the territory of the lord of Aizu, who gave me a demonstration of the unusual martial skills cherished by his samurai; not only can they swim while wearing suits of armour, but they can also operate bows as well. He even has a pond within the courtyard of his castle where his samurai practise. The secret of their technique lies in the strange jacket they wear over their suits of armour, which is made from a substance obtained from the bark of trees in countries such as Annam and Champa. It is called cork, and it floats in water without becoming saturated. I marvelled at the display in which a samurai sat upright in the pond – as if he was on an invisible horse – and loosed arrows at a target. By all means try this yourself, but practise using an old suit of armour. To risk rust appearing on a cherished family heirloom would be disgrace indeed.

5
Your Role in Guaranteeing a Harmonious Realm of Peace

It is clearly written in the Four Books and the Five Classics as well as in the military writings that in protecting the country, if one is ignorant of Learning he will be unable to govern.

IMAGAWA RYOSHUN, *REGULATIONS*

Now that we have covered armour, weapons and the martial arts, I am sure you are eager to learn about going to war, but please don't skip this chapter, because you must realize that much of your time will be taken up by the comparatively mundane and boring job of managing your domain, and it is vital that you get it right. You will not be able to control men on a battlefield if you cannot control them on a rice field.

How to Handle and Set an Example to the Lower Orders

As a samurai you will be expected to manage every aspect of life within the lands your lord has allotted to you. The larger the area of land, the greater will be the responsibilities and the more numerous the problems. Should you become a lord yourself, you will have the awesome task of ruling an entire province. In the olden days it was so easy. You just told the farmers what to do and beat them if they didn't do it; there could be no greater compliment than for it to be remarked that you were harsh with your peasants. Nowadays it is all very different. There are land surveys to complete, tax returns to maintain, record-keeping to do, storehouses to supervise, magistrates' duties to perform – not to mention organizing the clearing of dead bodies from the streets after a revenge raid, and suchlike. These tasks are difficult enough when you are in personal contact with your territories, but become almost impossible when a lord is forced to leave his province for several months, either to fight or to attend court in Edo. So how does a lord run his own territory while also serving the shogun in a personal capacity at one and the same time?

The answer is delegation. Select some junior person from among your samurai. Make him your senior counsellor or some such title, and let him run your domain while you go off to fight. He may well embezzle some of your money, but that's a small price to pay for the freedom to be a fighting warrior. While you are away, of course, you must not neglect your responsibility of setting an example to the lower classes. Rumours will quickly spread back to your domain if anyone observes you behaving in an unseemly fashion, and that would encourage rebellion and other unspeakable practices.

Tough on Crime, and Tough on the Causes of Crime

Let us begin with the maintenance of law and order. Sadly, there will be those within your domain who fail to appreciate both the excellent example you set them and also the need for them to display filial piety to a lord as to a father. Such evil fellows may turn to crime, and it will be your duty both to apprehend them and to punish them. Your task will be made immeasurably easier if you follow six simple rules that can make crime prevention a reality within your domain:

Rule One: Don't let them in

Why suffer from the carelessness of neighbours by allowing your province to become a place of sanctuary for their absconding felons? Make sure the entrances to your domain are closely guarded.

Rule Two: Don't tolerate Christianity

As I have said elsewhere, the pernicious religion of Christianity is almost an invitation to wrongdoing. These worthless wretches defy the wisdom of their betters, undermine the law of the gods and Buddhas and lay Japan open to the foreigners who would enslave us. Have no truck with them.

Rule Three: Prohibit gambling

Few pursuits seduce the lower orders into wasting their time so much as the despicable practice of gambling. Some people risk huge amounts on the fall of dice; others place wagers on the outcome of sumo wrestling bouts. If you can eradicate this evil then you will indeed have a peaceful domain.

Rule Four: Inform, inform, inform

The citizens of your domain must be made to realize that they have a duty to inform on anyone they suspect of breaking the law. To assist with this process you must make it clear to them that if they fail to disclose a culprit's whereabouts, then the felon's punishment will be inflicted upon them and their families instead. Few measures are better at bringing out the truth.

Rule Five: Support your local police

The maintenance of peace and order within your domain will be greatly facilitated if, following the example set in Edo by His Most Excellent Highness, you designate certain lower-ranking samurai as officers of the watch. These stout fellows not only act as reliable recipients for an informant's revelations, but also act as a visible and reassuring presence on our streets.

Rule Six: Understand the underlying causes of crime

It is very important to appreciate that many crimes have social origins, and that by understanding these contributory factors, misdemeanours may be prevented before they occur. So what are these social factors, and what can we do about them? In a nutshell, crime is committed by lewd and sordid persons who, through some failing in a previous existence, were not favoured with rebirth into the samurai class. As it is impossible for any of them to change this unfortunate status, they must be taught to respect both the property and the judgment of their superiors. If one of these persons commits a crime, is informed upon and confesses to the act, then a situation of harmony may be swiftly restored by his punishment. Problems arise only when a felon who is undoubtedly guilty fails to confess, because the only valid proof of guilt is the prisoner's own confession, taken down in writing and sealed by him. In this situation you are referred to the following section.

A Few Useful Tortures

If a felon fails to confess to a crime, torture is the only resort. These are presented here in order of increasing severity:

1 Scourging

A thorough beating with bamboo canes is usually sufficient to provoke a confession. If not, move on to:

When a samurai is placed in charge of lower-class persons he has to be prepared to exercise his authority. Strictness is essential, and so punishment such as this, a thorough beating of the buttocks, is sometimes thought necessary.

- - - - - - - - - - - - -

2 Hugging the stone

The criminal is made to kneel on a platform of sharp, three-cornered wooden batons in front of a pillar to which he is tied. Stone slabs are then placed across his thighs. Five should be ample to induce a confession, but ten are known to have been used on some stubborn persons.

When a criminal has failed to confess, the torture technique of the slabs (often called 'hugging the stone') should be sufficient to persuade him to admit his guilt.

3 The lobster

Allow the criminal's body to recover from hugging the stone (a few days should suffice) and then truss him up with his arms behind him and his legs in front. Take note of his skin colour, which over a few hours should change from red to purple to dark green. If it then passes to white his death is imminent, so the ropes should be untied.

A very stubborn criminal is tied up like a lobster to get him to confess. It is a tricky technique to use, because the felon may die before his admission of guilt.

The final method for persuading a criminal to confess is to suspend him from a rope and leave him there until he admits his crime. He can then be executed in the sure knowledge that justice has been done.

----

4 Suspension

Tie the criminal's arms behind him and hang him from a rope by the wrists. Leave him there for as long as it takes to evoke a confession.

Once a confession has been obtained your work is complete. The full legal process has been gone through and the criminal may now be executed. You will of course play no part in this unspeakable process, which will be handled by those who are scarcely human, but may withdraw, satisfied that you have assisted in bringing about the administration of justice. The streets of Japan will be that little bit safer because of your punctilious and merciful actions.

The Samurai's Own Behaviour

We now move on to the delicate question of your own behaviour, and there are certain situations when you must be particularly on your guard against temptation. Sadly, some members of the samurai class have been known to forget their exalted status and behave as if they were lewd and sordid persons. Such traitors to their class will suffer the most dreadful consequences, although in their case the ultimate penalty is always generously relaxed so that a samurai condemned to death may enjoy the Way of the Warrior by committing suicide instead of being executed. We are privileged indeed.

So where are you most at risk of losing your virtue? Well, the present need to provide guard duty for the shogun has meant that thousands of samurai like you have had to carry out long tours of duty in Edo since that city became our capital in 1603. When you are in Edo there is actually very little to do inside your lord's mansion except polish his armour ready for the march back to your castle-town in six months' time. You will therefore have time on your hands, and in Edo there are lots of people who will be more than ready to relieve you of your money or your life.

Much of a samurai's time in the days of peace is spent travelling the highways of Japan between one's castle-town and the shogun's capital of Edo.

I mention first the men called otokodate, which literally means 'chivalrous fellows'. This is far from being an accurate description. The otokodate are in fact lewd and sordid persons from the urban lower classes who have taken on airs that are totally inappropriate for someone from such a lowly position in society. They also carry swords. Yes, you read that correctly. They carry S-W-O-R-D-S. Sounds extraordinary, doesn't it? Did not Lord Toyotomi Hideyoshi in 1588 confiscate every sword in Japan that was not owned by a samurai, and then melt them all down to help make iron bolts for a great statue of Buddha he was building in Kyoto for the benefit of the nation? (Strictly speaking, he didn't actually melt any of them down but that's what he told the people he seized them from.) And is not the wearing of swords now confined only to the samurai class, as decreed by His Most Illustrious Highness? Indeed this is true, but in the seedy world of Edo, I am afraid, swords can be readily obtained, and these otokodate swagger about as if they were samurai, looking for trouble.

Whatever you do, do not accept a challenge to combat from one of these ruffians. Yes, your sword-fighting skills will be vastly superior to his, but these appalling persons never fight alone. Their idea of honourable single combat is to have you face one man while six others grab you from behind. My tips are to avoid dark alleys and not to get drunk, because it cannot be overemphasized that most assaults on samurai take place when the victim is intoxicated.

On the whole, the otokodate will leave you alone as long as you take sensible precautions, but of all the temptations that will come your way while on duty in Edo, one will appear – perhaps literally – knocking at your door. I think you can guess what I'm talking about. No, not geisha. You are unlikely to be able to hire a geisha on your stipend. I mean the ladies of the night in the Yoshiwara district of Edo. They will target you because you are a young man, a long way from home in a big city. Be warned, the vast majority of these women are infected with Chinese pox, a loathsome disease they pass on to any man who dallies with them. Despite the name, Chinese pox was brought to Japan by the Portuguese. Catch the pox and you will be leaving this world in unspeakable agony long before your time is due – and don't think you will be heading for the White Jade Pavilion. There will be no golden lotus to sit on where you are going. Instead, ghastly demons will tear the flesh from your bones with spiked forks.

It's just not worth it, is it?

Under the Tokugawa, a daimyo's family are required to live in Edo under the protection of the shogun. Ladies like these receive visits from their husbands once or twice a year.

Tobacco – Just Say No

When you are out on the streets of Edo enjoying the evening air you may be accosted by some rascal asking you to try something called tobacco. If approached in this way, there is one simple, golden rule: just say no. Tobacco is a deadly and addictive drug made from a noxious weed that is harvested, dried, cut into shreds and then fed into a small container called a pipe. The tobacco is then ignited and the smoke inhaled. How ridiculous it is! Like most evils in present-day Japan, tobacco has its origins overseas; of all the nefarious things brought here by the Portuguese (with the possible exceptions of Christianity and Chinese pox) there is no greater vice, no pursuit more injurious to the reputation of a samurai than the appalling practice of smoking tobacco. I understand that the tobacco plant grows naturally in a place called 'America'. Judging by the effects that tobacco produces on a person's behaviour, if ever we Japanese are unlucky enough to meet 'Americans' then we may reasonably expect them to be hopelessly addled and of no use to anyone. I have it on reliable authority that His Most Excellent Highness intends to ban tobacco. Once this is carried out, smoking will cease to exist.

6
Japan – The Land
of the Gods

Above all, believe in the gods and Buddhas.

HOJO SOUN, *TWENTY-ONE PRECEPTS*

✢ ✢ ✢

Japan is indeed the land of the gods. Since the dawn of creation they have protected us and made us the envy of lesser nations. The gods of Japan are all around, and their ways are closely interwoven with our lives; some scholars even describe our appreciation of the deities as Shinto – the Way of the Gods. Yet the ways of these divinities are mysterious indeed! Features such as a magnificent waterfall, a distant mountain or a strangely shaped rock all indicate the presence of a divine spirit, and – whoever they are – these gods require our constant attention. Most pleasing to the deities is to have special homes, which we call shrines, where they most generously agree to reside. Here we make offerings to them and they are pleased, rewarding us with good harvests. If these offerings are neglected, then such careless behaviour may arouse their anger. Typhoons will blow and battles will be lost.

Many centuries ago new gods came to Japan from China. At first there were those who saw this new religion, called Buddhism, as a threat to the gods of Japan, but good sense prevailed. Indeed the emperor (who after all was a living god) decreed that Buddhism was nothing to be feared and could reside harmoniously alongside our existing traditions. How wise he was, and how reassuring it is to see a Buddhist temple with a Shinto shrine built inside its courtyard. Confucianism is also

Japan is the land of the gods, and gods are to be found everywhere, especially enshrined within buildings like this one. This is a Shinto shrine, characterized by the presence of a torii (ceremonial gateway).

The Buddhist priesthood has an important role to play in society. A priest or monk will arrange a samurai's funeral and say prayers for the repose of his soul. Many brave priests are active on battlefields, supporting dying warriors.

very important to Japanese traditions. Earlier in this manual, reference was made to the way that our society is based upon Confucian principles: everyone knows his place and everyone is in his place. So the samurai of the lords pay filial piety to their masters, and they in turn behave like the children of the shogun. It is a harmonious situation indeed.

It is, however, a matter of infinite regret that less than 70 years ago a wicked new religion called Christianity came to Japan. It rapidly took root among the ignorant and the covetous, the latter – it must be said – included several otherwise noble lords, seduced by the lure of wealth and empty promises that accompanied it. Nowadays, thanks to the wisdom of His Most Excellent Highness, Christianity is banned; its churches have been destroyed and its priests have been expelled. The nuisance it caused had little to do with what Christians believe, which is of slight interest to anyone, but rather lies in the fact that its adherents have the power to form alliances hostile to the benevolent rule of His Most Excellent Highness – alliances supported by foreign armies, particularly those of Spain. It is for this reason that Christianity had to be eliminated, and we are much better off without it.

Among the gods honoured by samurai are these: the Seven Gods of Good Luck.

The Good Festival Guide

While being carried in your palanquin through a town or village, your ears may have on occasion caught the sound of raucous behaviour. On sliding the shutter to one side you may have chanced to observe a shrine festival in progress. This happens once or twice a year. The local villagers will carry through the streets an ornate portable shrine, wherein resides the god of the village. By these means the god is taken on a tour of his locality. There is much rejoicing, and people drink sake, dance, play musical instruments and eat squid-on-a-stick and octopus balls. All this is extremely vulgar behaviour, but can be tolerated because the farmers will consequently work that much harder for the remaining 364 days of the year. It is also an intangible part of our rich cultural heritage, of which you as a samurai are fortunate to be the chosen custodian. So why not get involved? Shrine festivals are not just for vulgar people to enjoy.

Ghosts and Other Strange Beings – What You Need To Know

I now mention the controversial topic of ghosts, goblins and other strange beings. Why controversial? Because certain ignorant people will tell you that such sprites do not exist. How misguided they are! Let me give you one very clear proof. You may have noticed that certain people from the lower classes tend to defecate in the street. Come back a few days later and the excrement is no longer there. No one will have touched it, so where has it gone? It has been eaten by hungry ghosts. What other explanation can there be? These revolting yet invisible creatures therefore perform a useful function.

Listing the enormous variety of supernatural creatures that exist would fill this entire book, so I will restrict myself to those that a samurai is most likely to encounter in the course of his daily life. If out late at night you may meet Bakemono Tofu, the ghostly bean-curd seller. If you speak to him you will die. Then there is the dreadful goblin Hitotsume Kozo, who is tall, white-skinned and thin; with one eye and long arms from which the flesh sags. He wears a large sedge hat on top of straggly white hair, while a distended stomach protrudes over his loin-cloth. Hitotsume Kozo carries a ball of fire in a sieve; it is indescribable.

Other extraordinary beings include household objects that come to life on their 100th birthday. Particularly notorious are the straw-sandal ghosts, which are old pairs of footwear that suddenly start running around the house screaming. Kappa (beings with the body of a tortoise, the limbs of a frog and the head of a monkey) inhabit ponds and are fond of attacking women. If you should meet a kappa, there is a well-established means of getting rid of it. Being an aquatic creature, the kappa requires water to sustain its life, and when on dry land a small quantity is retained within the shallow depression on top of its head. Fortunately, all kappa are extremely polite, so instead of running away in terror you should bow to it. The kappa will then return your bow, and as it does so the water will run out. The kappa will then collapse and you will have it at your mercy.

Samurai believe that there are many strange beings about. These yokai include demons, ghosts and goblins. The pictured example is a tengu, which are greatly to be feared because of their prowess at sword-fighting.

The fierce tengu live in forests. They have bodies that are half-human and half-crow, and they are very good at sword-fighting. Other mischievous beings look much more ordinary. Foxes, as is well known, possess supernatural powers to an almost limitless degree, and frequently delude men by assuming the form of a beautiful woman. The man is captivated, seduced and ultimately destroyed. The ghosts of dead warriors can also be quite intimidating; particularly in those cases when it was your army that turned them into ghosts in the first place. Most mysterious noises and strange lights near the sites of ruined castles can be explained by the presence of the spirits of dead samurai. They rarely seek revenge; rather they are wandering souls, more to be pitied than feared. The only example I know of ghostly samurai attacking living ones occurred on the site of the famous battle of Dan no Ura in 1185.

ABOVE *Mori Sanzaemon Yoshinari (1523–70), a samurai lord in the service of Oda Nobunaga, carries a wounded comrade on his back. Yoshinari was killed fighting for Nobunaga against the Asai and Asakura at the battle of Anegawa in 1570.*

OVERLEAF *The battle of Shizugatake (1583) is shown on this folding screen. The samurai of Toyotomi Hideyoshi, who have appeared in the valley, are now engaging the troops of Sakuma Morimasa, who have left the safety of their siege lines.*

ABOVE *At the Battle of Shizugatake, Kato Kiyomasa, one of the 'Seven Spears' overcomes his opponent using a ju-jutsu hold, only for both of them fall off the narrow mountain path.*

OPPOSITE *The red-clad samurai of the Ii clan attack Kimura Shigenari during the summer campaign of Osaka. Note the sashimono flags on their backs, one of which is being held by an attendant as his master fights an individual combat.*

Kusunoki Masashige, the epitome of samurai loyalty, pledges his service to Emperor Go-Daigo in his bid to overthrow the Hojo regency and restore the imperial power. Masashige, who was to lose his life at the battle of Minatogawa in 1336, fought on behalf of the emperor and against his own better judgment.

Ishikawa Hyosuke Kazumitsu (1565–83), who was killed at the battle of Shizugatake in 1583, is shown here with arrows sticking out of his armour. Brave even in defeat, Kazumitsu here represents the essence of the samurai.

So great was the slaughter of the Taira family's samurai that the sea ran red with the blood of the slain and the dye from the Taira's flags. Taira Tomomori, the Taira commander, committed suicide by tying himself to an anchor and jumping into the sea. A few years later, Tomomori and his dead samurai rose up out of the deep to challenge a Minamoto ship that was making its way through the nearby straits of Shimonoseki.

Going on Pilgrimage – Should I or Shouldn't I?

If, in pursuit of your noble samurai duties, you travel through the more remote mountainous areas of Japan, or pass a small wayside shrine out in the countryside, you may well notice people standing around clad in white, carrying staves and wearing large straw hats. They are on pilgrimage. The idea is to gain spiritual merit by visiting a place, or a series of places, that have particular religious connotations. Popular examples of pilgrimage destinations include the Great Shrine of Ise (the home of Amaterasu, Goddess of the Sun and the Divine Ancestress of our Emperor) and Shikoku Island, where each year thousands of pilgrims walk between the various temples associated with Saint Kobo Daishi of the Shingon sect.

To undertake a pilgrimage around a series of holy places is a worthy pursuit. Many spiritual benefits might accrue as a result of such unselfish endeavours.

The question many samurai ask is 'Should I join them?' They naturally fear that the undoubted religious benefits that they will accrue from making a pilgrimage could be outweighed by having to associate with lewd and sordid persons. I reply that they need not worry: just because a samurai is in close proximity to a lower-class person does not mean that he is somehow soiled – his virtue and breeding will always show through. So by all means go on pilgrimage to learn at first-hand about the impermanence of all phenomena, and much good may it do you.

First you will have to acquire your pilgrim's garb, which is white, the colour of mourning. (Insist that the seller gives you a guarantee of impermanence.) The wide-brimmed hat will shield you from the sun and also conceal your identity, should you still have qualms on that score. You will also need a stout wooden staff. The true pilgrim refuses to carry food, relying on the generosity of others to feed him. Be wary: this could be a little tricky if you pass through an area that your army has recently devastated.

The one caveat I would add to this general seal of approval about making pilgrimages concerns yamabushi (mountain ascetics), whose company should be avoided at all costs – not that you are likely to be invited anyway. For the yamabushi, pilgrimage forms only a small part of their unusual religious practices, which include divination, fortune telling and faith healing. Dressed in funereal white robes, the yamabushi make journeys through the mountains, blowing mournful sounds from their shell trumpets. On their travels they perform austerities that renew their magical power to carry out exorcisms and the like. These exacting rituals include being suspended by the legs over a cliff as they confess their sins, being confined within a smoke-filled room, and bathing naked under an icy waterfall. Small wonder that most samurai consider them to be mad.

7
The Cultivated Samurai

One should put forth effort in matters of learning.

KATO KIYOMASA, *PRECEPTS*

✜ ✜ ✜

As a samurai, you will be expected to set an example to the lower orders as much by your sensitivity to artistic matters and cultural pursuits as by your firm discipline at home and self-sacrificing behaviour on the battlefield. The first question that any samurai who wishes to cultivate himself in this way is likely to ask is 'When do I find the time?' How indeed, amid the hurly-burly of a samurai's busy life, can he ever hope to isolate that precious moment of stillness?

The answer is closely related to the practice of Zen. Even though I adhere to the tenets of Pure Land Buddhism, I have always recognized that Zen possesses great treasures, many of which are to be found in tranquillity. The composure that allows the samurai to face the prospect of death in battle is also achievable in art, where Zen principles allow the busy samurai warrior to separate himself from the noise around and enter into the aesthetic sphere. Having acquired that moment of stillness the samurai must make a judgment as to how he might best fill it, because some forms of popular artistic expression and entertainment are unspeakably vulgar. The cultivated samurai must therefore exert a considerable degree of discretion when deciding which art forms are acceptable for his dignified indulgence. In this section I have selected a number of suitable categories, which I present to you with carefully considered notes of caution.

Toyotomi Hideyoshi, the unifier of Japan, shown here in armour and playing a sho. Musical prowess is unusual among samurai but is greatly admired.

The Samurai's Essential Reading List

True artistic sensibilities can be realized only by years of dedicated practice, but much useful information – about both art and the entire spectrum of samurai behaviour – may be gleaned from great works of literature. The most important of all are the gunkimono (war tales). Written centuries ago, they tell the epic story of how our ancestors lived, fought and died. These are best appreciated when chanted to you by a blind itinerant monk within the confines of your lord's castle. If this is not possible, then seat yourself comfortably and open the pages of these great tales. You may well be moved to tears as you read the tragic and moving stories therein.

My particular favourite is *Heike Monogatari*, which relates how the Taira family, who succumbed to overweening pride, were vanquished by the Minamoto family during the Gempei War (1180–85). It describes battles very beautifully as encounters between magnificent samurai warriors, where individual challenges are made to seek out only the noblest of opponents. A single combat then takes place, with no other fighters allowed to join in, and woe betide any vulgar person who spoils the situation by shooting one of the adversaries dead with an arrow! *Heike Monogatari* is sublime and uplifting, and must be highly recommended to any young samurai who wishes to emulate the deeds of his ancestors, for here they are in all their glorious details. For something more up to date, may I recommend *Taiheiki*, a glorious tale of the wars of the 14th century. In both you will find unerring and inspiring examples on which to base your own future behaviour.

It is, however, for similar reasons that young samurai should be actively discouraged from reading rubbish such as *Mutsu Waki*. This notorious chronicle of the samurai wars in northern Japan during the 11th century dwells on military matters in a most unseemly manner. Its pages are filled with unbelievable nonsense suggesting that samurai set fire to buildings and cut down those who tried to flee, or that noble warriors could even be killed by vulgar persons. Leaving aside the fact that these accounts are true, such works should find no place within your castle's library.

By contrast, poetry is something that all samurai should be encouraged to read and write. Every samurai should be skilled at composing poems, particularly when he is performing the tea ceremony or about to disembowel himself. But care should be taken when selecting which poems to read, as many are written by courtiers who know nothing of the real world, and reading them can weaken the spirit. Novels are to be avoided too, because most of them are written by women.

- - - - - - - - - - - - - - - -
Poetry is seen as a fitting accomplishment for a samurai to value and enjoy. Not only should he read poetry, but he should also compose verses, particularly when at a tea ceremony or preparing to disembowel himself.

Theatrical Entertainment and the Sensitive Samurai

Many young samurai ask me 'Should I attend theatrical performances, and, if so, which ones?' My answer is that there is only one form of theatrical performance sufficiently dignified for the samurai class, and this is the classical Noh theatre. All other forms are sordid and vulgar, so say 'Yes' only to Noh.

The finest Noh performances are given by masters of the art, who have imbibed the tradition of centuries. Masked and robed, they will transport you to another realm. The subject matter of most Noh plays is very similar to that of the war tales, and so watching a Noh play is like seeing *Heike Monogatari* come to life. You will be entranced by the spectacle as the ghost of a dead warrior appears at the edge of the stage and moves to its centre, taking a full half-hour to do so. Such suspense! And what could compare to the drama inherent in the pursuit of the Earth Spider? Unmissable!

I must, however, introduce a warning, because there has been a new form of theatre recently introduced to Edo called Kabuki. It is popular with merchants and other lewd and sordid persons. At first sight it looks very similar to the Noh theatre, but there are profound differences that I believe make Kabuki a serious threat to the stability of society and a practice injurious to the morals of the samurai class. After considerable pressure from colleagues I went to see a Kabuki performance and was thoroughly shocked. None of the actors wore a mask, and the plot was not about a dignified warrior encountering ghosts and dying honourably (as might be expected from something that will watched by the impressionable lower classes). Rather it concerned a samurai family of the present day, and the difficulties they were experiencing while going about their noble duties in conformity with the Confucian teachings about filial piety. That such lower-class persons should dare to enact upon a public stage a matter about which they can have no understanding is an affront to public morality. Worst of all, at one point in the play the actor playing the head of the household (to whom the other household members should have been paying the utmost respect) pretends to trip over a bucket, at which the audience laughed. At this point I walked out in disgust.

In time, I hope, His Most Excellent Highness may be persuaded to ban this affront to public decency that holds the samurai class in such contempt.

Ink Painting for Pleasure and Profit

Would you be willing to try your hand at an art form enjoyed by one of the greatest swordsmen of our age? I am sure you would, so why not try painting with black ink? Painting – I hear you ask – is that not a pursuit suitable only for perfumed courtiers? No it is not, because this art form is practised by no less a person than the great swordsman Miyamoto Musashi, whom you may have encountered during one of his frequent warrior pilgrimages. Like most kengo (master swordsman) of his ilk, Miyamoto Musashi travels the country seeking suitable opponents, whom he challenges and frequently kills. After such a bout he will retire to a nearby temple and produce a quick ink painting. The absence of colour ensures the absence of vulgarity, so why not try it yourself? You don't actually have to kill someone before you begin.

Football – The Beautiful Game

Kemari (football) is a gentle pastime dating back centuries. Courtiers may be seen playing it within the wisteria-covered gardens of the imperial palace. Some samurai have been known to indulge a passion for football, and even the great samurai commander Oda Nobunaga was fond of it.

Kemari (football) is a game that can be enjoyed by samurai as much as by courtiers. Here we see a practitioner kicking the deerskin ball into the air within the precincts of a shrine.

If you fancy a game but are a little nervous about it then remember that all football players come under the benevolent protection of Mari no kami, the three-headed god of football, so there is very little to worry about. First of all you will require a voluminous silk robe, a stiffened black hat, and heavy, lacquered clogs. You then join up with seven samurai comrades who are suitably immersed in the aesthetic sensibilities of the game. Make your way with them to the meticulously raked gravel courtyard of a shrine or palace. A Shinto priest will say prayers of exorcism over a ball made from deerskin. Everyone bows, and the game commences.

The idea is that the ball is kicked from one player to another with the aim of keeping it in the air at all times. That's really all there is to it, but the overall effect is exceedingly harmonious. As the players kick the ball they comment on the changing of the seasons, or the melancholy fall of cherry blossom, and generously applaud when one of their fellow players performs a particularly artful or aesthetically pleasing move. It is indeed a beautiful game!

No board game is better for learning strategy than go. Here we see two samurai enjoying the classic trial of cunning.

Board Games

Sometimes it is pleasant to spend the evening in, and a board game is the perfect way to enjoy a friend's company. Some games, unfortunately, have associations with gambling, and so anything involving the roll of dice is to be avoided. How much better it is to play shogi, where the pieces stand like two armies of tiny samurai arranged for combat. But better still is a game of go. Shogi may be a battle, but go is total war. One by one you place your white or black stones on the intersecting lines of the board until the territory they surround becomes your own and your opponent's stones vanish from sight. If hunting provides training for a samurai, then go provides training for a general.

Gardening – How to Get the Best Out Of Your Rocks

What a joy to the eyes is the traditional Japanese garden. Much of the art of these enclosures takes its inspiration from the aesthetics of Zen, where things are suggested rather than stated openly. The quintessential example of this is to construct a garden consisting only of rocks and sand that will express the transient nature of created phenomena.

Whole books have been written about Japanese garden design, so I will confine myself to just a few elements that I believe provide the key to its understanding. The selection of one's rocks is all-important. They must possess beauty and harmony, but I think it is going too far to covet a particular rock just because it was once stained by the blood of a dead samurai – as is the case of a certain rock in the garden of the Daigoji in Kyoto. The placing of the rocks will take time and much effort, but this diagram may help by providing suggestions about how three differently shaped stones may be harmoniously combined. You will then wish to add other elements, perhaps a pond, or why not use the kare-sansui technique, whereby the flow of water, even a mighty torrent, is merely suggested? Once you move on to larger compositions such as this an overall plan is useful, so perhaps consider how a garden involving both a hill and a water feature might look. Finally, do not neglect the possibilities afforded by shakkei (borrowed scenery). Many of the great temple gardens of Kyoto make use of the distant view of the hills of Higashiyama, or just an aesthetically pleasing bamboo grove next door. Adjoining trees, bushes and even the sides of cliffs on adjacent properties may all be brought to bear when creating your harmonious composition. It certainly helps if you have friendly and cooperative neighbours.

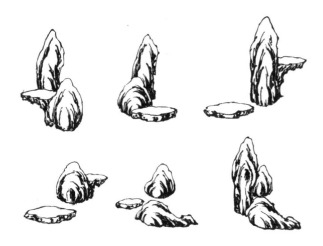

Garden design is the perfect accomplishment for a cultivated samurai.
This illustration shows various arrangements that can be made using only
three rocks. All are exceedingly harmonious.

The Tea Ceremony – Dos and Don'ts

There is no pursuit in all Japan more exquisite, more harmonious or more soothing to the mind than the tea ceremony. Nothing better expresses Japanese culture than to sit in a tea house with the kettle bubbling away, caressing a rare tea bowl, admiring the seasonal flowers of the garden, composing poetry by the light of a harvest moon – simply appreciating the transient nature of all human existence.

The sequence of events in a typical tea ceremony is quite straightforward, and its own simplicity says much about the exquisite nature of the practice. Your guests will assemble in the waiting bower. They will be greeted by the tea master, who will escort them into the tea house. The tea master then enters by a different, knee-high door, thereby showing his humility. The charcoal fire is kindled and water is boiled. With the grace born of years of dedicated practice, the tea master adds the water to the matcha (powdered green tea) and stirs it to a froth. The tea is then drunk. Alas, this bare description cannot do justice to the peerlessness of the entire performance: the admiration of the fine tea bowl; the appreciation of the harmony of the decor and its relationship to the current season; the sharing of conversation and poetry; the experience of stillness.

But to achieve this, the tea ceremony has to be done properly. There are many traps for the unwary, so here are a few dos and don'ts.

DO use a qualified tea master

It takes years to become a master of tea. By all means practise on your friends, but for a really impressive ceremony you must hire someone who is already expert. Leave all the organization to him. You will be admired all the more for your decision to employ him than for any risky ritual that you may yourself have planned.

A samurai kneeling in his formal civilian costume with one sword at his side.

DO choose flowers that are seasonal

A good tea ceremony should reflect the season in which it is performed, so don't go out of your way to obtain fruits or flowers that are out of season in your part of Japan. It looks vulgar.

DO select exquisite pottery

Your tea master will of course own some priceless tea bowls and cha-ire (tea caddies), but don't expect him to bring them along to your humble abode. Instead, try to build up your own stock of beautiful ceramics.

These need not cost a fortune. Korean tea vessels are much prized, but prices have come down considerably since we allowed prisoners of war from the Korean invasion to stay in Japan and set up kilns. Karatsu is an excellent place to look for a bargain tea bowl, and don't miss the opportunity to buy a cha-ire in green celadon.

DO ensure that monsters are kept at bay

As the tea ceremony is usually performed out of doors, there is the ever-present danger that a monster may turn up. Tengu and kappa particularly lurk in wooded surroundings, and may be tempted to cause mischief. The simplest way to prevent this is to make an offering to them and then place a notice by your garden gate asking them to keep away. I do this every time and have never had a tea ceremony spoiled by a monster.

DON'T overdo the decoration

It may seem unnecessary to make this point about a ritual that involves restraint and harmony, but there can be an unfortunate tendency among samurai to try and outdo each other in the exquisiteness of the surroundings in which the tea ceremony will take place. A simple hut is all you need. Lord Toyotomi Hideyoshi – it is true – had a tea room where the interior was covered in gold leaf, but this is getting very close to vulgarity.

DON'T smash your tea bowls

Matsunaga Hisahide smashed his priceless tea bowls before committing suicide. Please note that this was a special case and an exceptional situation. Displays of temper during a tea ceremony are also totally unacceptable. If you spill scalding tea on your lap remember that the Way of the Warrior requires a display of self-control.

DON'T commit murder during a tea ceremony

Unfortunately there have been many instances of people abusing the tea ceremony by exploiting it as cover for a clandestine meeting, or even for carrying out an assassination. Quite apart from the mess, few things destroy the composure and harmony of a tea ceremony more effectively than to have one of the guests murdered.

When the battle is over, samurai can relax in the bathhouse and make themselves presentable to serve their lord once again.

In conclusion, the samurai who embraces the ways of art and peace as skilfully as he embraces the ways of war may be likened to a cart that has two wheels on its axle and thus runs straight in the service of his lord. May you be diligent in both!

8
The Samurai as Military Commander

There is a saying of the ancients that goes, 'It is painful to hear the gong commanding a retreat, but a joy to hear one that sounds the advance.'

TAKEDA NOBUSHIGE, *OPINIONS IN NINETY-NINE ARTICLES*

One day, if you have studied really well, practised the martial arts assiduously, shown leadership qualities on your estates and obeyed your betters in accordance with the tenets of filial piety, you will be given the military command of others. Some of them will be samurai like you, so it is vital that you learn how to command an army, and how to earn respect both on the battlefield and off it.

Raising an Army in Three Easy Steps

In the olden days, your first duty as commander would have been to raise an army. This is less important nowadays because we are all basking in the martial virtue of His Most Excellent Highness, and our armies of professional samurai are effectively in a state of permanent readiness. There may be occasions, however, when further troops have to be assembled from among one's followers. The following section describes the traditional method by which this is done.

Step One

The most important point is that you should know long before you begin raising an army exactly what is required from you and from your men in terms of numbers and equipment. As to the size of your contingent, this will be on a sliding scale dependent upon your personal wealth as measured by the yield of your rice fields in koku (which, you will recall from an earlier section is the amount of rice considered necessary to feed one man for one year). Today, of course, you are more likely to receive a monetary stipend of equivalent value from the lord, who receives the tax rice from the farmers and stores it, but the principle is the same. By and large you will be required to supply one mounted and twenty unmounted samurai and ashigaru (foot soldiers) for every hundred koku of your assessed income. If you are a samurai of modest means, then the horseman will probably be you. Your followers will consist of half a dozen fully armoured samurai with swords and spears, and three or four ashigaru in personal attendance upon you as bodyguards (a groom, a spear-carrier and the like); the balance of your manpower requirements will most likely be made up of ashigaru armed with arquebuses, spears or bows. When you present your contingent to your lord it will probably be the case that these latter ashigaru will be taken and allocated to the large weapon squads under the command of another. Depending on your rank you may have command of men such as these. Otherwise you may fight in a samurai unit, or even have higher responsibilities of command and organization.

Step Two

If you have taken the sensible precaution of ascertaining who your troops are, you will be better prepared when the call to arms arrives. The muster may have originated in an outpost located on the borders of the province, with a series of fire beacons communicating to your castle-town that there is an emergency. Perhaps your province is about to be raided by a hostile neighbour? Or could it be that His Most Excellent Highness requires urgent reinforcements for a campaign? If your province lies on the island of Kyushu the warning could even herald an invasion from China. Whatever the nature of the alarm, you must always be ready to respond.

On the battlefield, a unit of samurai are identified by the sashimono (back flags) that they wear in common. High-ranking samurai are allowed to wear individual sashimono bearing their own mon (badges) or even their names.

- - - - - - - - -

Step Three

In the olden days, getting your army together could be an exciting and nerve-wracking process. Many of the men would have been part-time farmer-samurai, and it was said of the Chosokabe family of Shikoku Island that they were so ready to fight, that they tended to their rice crop with their spears stuck into the field boundaries and a spare pair of sandals tied to their weapon. The question of muster and march has recently become much more straightforward, because most of the samurai under your command will already be stationed in the castle. Many foot soldiers will also be there, so only a minority will need to be summoned from the fields. Send out runners to fetch them and order someone to beat the drum in the castle tower. Word will soon get around. When everyone is assembled, fully kitted out and inspected, you and your men are ready to march off in the service of your lord.

The Command of Armies – Who Does What?

In the bygone days it was always the lord himself who led his army into battle. During the time of the great civil wars, when battles sometimes occurred simultaneously, the lord usually delegated command of his army to his most loyal general, but the ultimate burden of responsibility always fell upon one man. One day it could be you – but don't worry, because you will be assisted and indeed protected by the tightly knit group who stand beside the commander-in-chief. They are called the hatamoto (under the standard).

Control of troops on a battlefield is exercised either by the daimyo (lord) himself or by the trusted and experienced samurai general he has appointed to be his commander-in-chief.

The majority of a lord's hatamoto act as a personal escort, forming his elite Horse Guards and Foot Guards. Men from these units are always superbly attired in gorgeous armour, splendid flags and tend to wear a horo (a large, balloon-like cloak that you may have seen being worn by the highest-ranking samurai). The horo denotes a superlative warrior and often also worn by the Courier Guards, who take messages from the commander to different units of the army. These brave men have to be easily recognizable, so a brilliantly and distinctively coloured horo is a splendid uniform for them to wear as they gallop to and fro across the battlefield.

One day you may be invited to join the select group of the hatamoto. If it happens that you are closely related to the lord then you will surely already be among them, and if you are the son of one of his most loyal retainers and have acted as your lord's page then you will also probably 'stand under the flag' as a matter of course. Otherwise it is only through the performance of great deeds on the battlefield, coupled with rigorous adherence to the doctrines of filial piety, that you will enter the ranks of the greatest fighters to have embraced the Way of the Warrior.

Please, do not make the assumption that being a hatamoto samurai is solely about fighting. Much organization goes on behind the scenes, and this is the responsibility of certain illustrious warriors within the hatamoto who have taken on comparatively mundane – but no less honourable – tasks. These men are the bugyo, to whom your lord has delegated responsibilities such as being in charge of the supply of armour and weapons; overseeing river transport; the recording of honourable deeds; and discipline within the army, as well as more obviously military roles, for example tactical planning. Certain skilled and experienced bugyo will be your lord's strategic advisers. The famous Yamamoto Kansuke, who was killed in 1561 at the fourth battle of Kawanakajima, was Takeda Shingen's leading strategist. Others have a gift for organizing things and keeping records, and all this is very honourable.

Apart from the bugyo, the other samurai who have clearly defined leadership roles are the taisho – generals who will command different units on the battlefield. If, as I envisage, you are one day serving in a unit of mounted samurai, then a taisho will be your commander. It is he who will watch for the lowering of the lord's war fan, and then order you forwards in an exciting charge with spears readied. Your taisho will be a very brave man, for it is he who will lead that surge into battle and disappear within the smoke to take many heads.

Some junior samurai will act as the personal attendants to his lordship. They groom his horse, carry his weapons and see to his personal needs. The bravest of these men are the helmet bearer and standard bearers. These simple fellows will carry the banners and other devices that proclaim to an enemy that the lord is present, thus acting almost as an invitation to the enemy to open fire. Most of these men are eventually promoted to high samurai rank, if they live long enough.

The Successful Deployment of Vulgar Persons

Not every taisho will command other samurai, because the majority of fighting men in your army will be ashigaru, all of whom (apart from the personal attendants previously noted) will be organized into weapon squads. Years ago there were many samurai who turned their noses up at the idea of having command over lower-class fighting men. They thought it was beneath their dignity. Well, they had a point, and I am sufficiently old-fashioned to appreciate this opinion – but we must all move with the times. I would be the first to acknowledge that the era of peace we now enjoy (thanks to the martial virtues of Their Most Illustrious and Excellent Highnesses, the shogun and his father) could not have been achieved without the command exercised by the noble samurai who swallowed their pride and accepted humbly their duty to direct vulgar persons. Among the ranks of the hatamoto, therefore, are some very noble samurai who have the title 'General of Ashigaru'. They are certainly not ashamed of it, and neither should you be.

Your average ashigaru in the weapon squads is a rough chap, but he will fight well under the right leader. Indeed, this is the key to success: leadership and strict discipline are the factors that have transformed the ashigaru units from a casually recruited rabble (motivated largely by loot and readily absconding) into what one must now recognize as being the lower ranks of the samurai class. To a very great extent this is due to the foresight of Oda Nobunaga, Lord of Owari, the ally and friend of His Most Illustrious Highness until his tragic death in 1582.

I have had command of ashigaru, and have found them to be jolly good fellows, not to be despised. Why, even Lord Toyotomi Hideyoshi, who re-unified Japan, started out as an ashigaru before becoming one of the most brilliant generals Japan has ever produced. He was skilled in administration, a fine master of tea ceremonies and a superlative leader of men – what's more, his generals would have followed him into hell itself.

How to Fire an Arquebus

The ashigaru are organized according to the weapon groups of arque-buses, bows and spears. The first two groups may be taken together, as they are both missile weapons. Ashigaru archers are likely to be as skilled as samurai archers, if not more so, because the practice of archery has declined somewhat among the better classes over the years. The ashigaru bowmen, however, operate their weapons from foot, not on horseback, and will most frequently be required to loose arrows in volleys, instead of selecting an honourable target. Alas, such is the impersonal state of war today! Some ashigaru may be selected as sharpshooters, and go on to practise their archery in a manner that is more distinguished.

Unlike the archers, whose expertise requires skill and constant practice, the men with arquebuses need only drill and discipline, and as the firearms squads will be the largest of the three groups it is vital you know how one of these fiendish devices works. I am not, of course, sug-gesting that you will be required to fire an arquebus on the battlefield – that would be well below your exalted status – but there may well be instances when you are placed in command of vulgar persons, who will look to you for example, inspiration and leadership in the confusion of battle. It is therefore vitally important that you are aware of the steps that must be drilled into the foot soldiers, so they know exactly what they are doing in the heat of conflict.

The introduction of firearms from Europe in 1543 transformed Japanese warfare. This weapon is a matchlock musket, which are best fired in volleys. Strict discipline is needed to ensure this works effectively.

- - - - - - - - - - - - - - - - - -

The arquebus (a weapon introduced by the Portuguese) is a complex device, made dangerous for the operator because of the lighted match that is ever present, ready to ignite the charge. The first rule is that the match must always be kept away from the pan until the command has been given to fire.

Step One

Begin by lining up your ashigaru and commanding them to kneel. At this stage the match may be ignited using tinder and allowed to smoulder. The best way of keeping it well clear of the arquebus, but still close enough to be reached, is to loop it through the hole conveniently located in the weapon's stock.

Step Two

The powder flask is now taken up, and a small quantity of gunpowder is tipped into the muzzle. The ramrod is applied and the charge driven home. The bullet may now be introduced. It too is carefully rammed down the barrel.

Step Three

The pan cover may now be slid to one side, and more powder inserted into the holder. Close the cover. This is MOST important, because now the lighted and smouldering end of the match will be inserted into the serpentine (cock) that has been pulled back.

Step Four

Having inserted the match and cocked the serpentine, the end of the match is blown upon to bring it most fully to life. The gun is then lifted to the horizontal position so that aiming may be carried out. Only now is the pan cover reopened.

Step Five

The order 'Fire' will be given, at which the trigger is pulled, the powder ignited and the bullet sent forcefully on its way. If you are using an ozutsu (the very heavy calibre version of the arquebus) the recoil will be so great that an inexperienced gunner will probably fall flat on his back, to the amusement of all.

This picture shows the larger version of the arquebus, known as the ozutsu (hand cannon). The recoil from one of these weapons is tremendous. They are customarily fired at quite high elevations to reach the rear ranks of an enemy army.

The Spearmen - Every General's Nightmare

Ask any general which weapon group gives him the most headaches and he will reply 'The spearmen'. This is not because they are exceptionally wilful or cowardly, but because (unlike the missile squads, which discharge their weapons and then retire) the spearmen must take a stand and unflinchingly endure all the bullets and arrows that the enemy may fire at them. In battle the spearmen may be required to form an impenetrable hedge; or execute a slow but steady advance while keeping order in their ranks. When you remember that some of these spears can be as long as the combined height of four men, you will appreciate how difficult it is to carry out, let along orchestrate, such manoeuvres. In Europe, I believe, they have similar soldiers called 'pikemen' – and also very similar problems.

The spearmen squads in a samurai army are a vital tool, but very difficult to control. Drill is essential if these unwieldy blocks of men are to be made to move in unison.

The greatest challenge concerning the spearmen is the difficulty involved in getting them to move in unison. If you are not careful then gaps will appear in their ranks, and a vigilant enemy may take advantage of the disorder to cause utter havoc with a cavalry charge. One final point: when your spearmen are on the march, do make sure that they all slip scabbards over their spear blades, otherwise severe accidents might result.

Using Warriors from Outside – Quantity or Quality?

In this section I pose the perfectly serious question: can you have too many fighting men? A large army may impress and intimidate your enemy, but of what does it consist? Is your army made up of samurai and ashigaru who display loyalty in accordance with the tenets of filial piety, or have they been casually recruited like the ashigaru of a century ago, simply to make up the numbers?

A Bearers, Porters and Coolies in General

Amazing as it may seem, up to six out of every ten men in your army, marching off to war, may not actually be fighting troops. A modern army requires a great deal of equipment, so recruiting people to carry it is unavoidable. If a relationship of trust is developed over a period of time then these men may be given a simple uniform jacket and a basic helmet to wear, though very often it is a case of grabbing whoever is available when the call to arms arrives. There may be discipline problems with them, but a good thrashing always works wonders.

B Recruiting Ronin – Some Useful Advice

It is often tempting to increase the size of your army by recruiting ronin (men of the waves). These are samurai who have lost their masters, and therefore have no one to fight for. There is no reason why they should not be integrated into your army and provide loyal service, but do take care. Some may just be rascals who have assumed the identities of dead samurai; what's more their ranks can conceal criminals or absconders hiding past misdemeanours. These vagabonds can appear very plausible, because all ronin are desperate for employment in an established army as a lord's samurai. Men of the waves can make very good fighters, but be sure to run thorough background checks before taking them on.

⊂ Ninja: A Value-for-Money Guide

At this stage I feel compelled to deal with the sordid subject of hiring ninja. Ninja are assassins, spies and subversives trained in ninjutsu – the art of stealth and invisibility. Their trade is underhand; their cover is darkness and disguise. A ninja's loyalty is not to a lord, but to the money that he receives for killing noble samurai like you; warriors of the sort they would never dare to meet face to face in a proper fight. Their weapon is the knife in the dark, the slow-acting poison, the deadly magic curse or the sudden strangulation on a castle wall. This is so different from the way we operate. For example, is there a samurai anywhere in Japan who does not desire above all things to be the first into a battle? Yet how dismayed would you be to discover that a ninja had already entered the enemy position, assassinated their commander and caused the army to surrender before you could even draw your own noble sword. How mortifying! How vulgar! So let us have nothing to do with ninja. If we are to achieve victory, let it be nobly won – while taking precautions so that you do not yourself become a victim of their despicable craft. Remember always that the way of the ninja is not the same as the Way of the Warrior. Take heed!

The secret assassins known as ninja are an ever-present danger, but if a lord takes sensible precautions he has very little to fear from them.

D Warrior Monks – Who Exactly Are They?

Every now and then you will cut off an enemy samurai's head, from which all the hair has been shaved. Your companions will be likely to say, 'That's a warrior monk,' but what does this expression actually mean? The simplest explanation is that the samurai you have killed is indeed a monk, or more likely a priest, but has carried on being a samurai at the same time. In other words, he has been ordained as a member of the Buddhist clergy, but has neither entered a monastery nor given up fighting to run a temple. Take for example my personal situation: I am a priest of the Pure Land sect, and so have a shaven head, though I wouldn't go so far as to call myself a warrior monk.

This picture shows the original sohei (warrior monks). These men were recruited to defend the temples of Nara and Mount Hiei during the 10th century. Many were armed with naginata.

Many centuries ago there were entire armies of real warrior monks that were fielded by the great Temples of Mount Hiei (near Kyoto) and Nara. Until only a few years ago the Negorodera Temple in Kii province maintained its own army before being crushed by Lord Toyotomi Hideyoshi in 1585. 'But what of the Ikko-ikki?' I hear you ask, 'Their armies consist of fanatical Buddhists, so are they warrior monks?' Certainly not! The Ikko-ikki are a peasant rabble of religious extremists, who have dared to question the all-encompassing wisdom and martial virtue of the samurai class in general, and certain noble lords in particular. They are even worse than Christians, being motivated by a very misguided attachment to the True Pure Land sect (a heretical offshoot of my own Pure Land sect). A few decades ago they presumed to rebel against His Most Illustrious Highness in Mikawa province and were utterly chastised. Other armies of these sordid and despicable characters then defied Lord Oda Nobunaga, who crushed them utterly in 1580. If peasant revolts (religious or otherwise) occur in your domain then you must do likewise.

4
The Samurai on the Battlefield

Having been born into the house of a warrior, one's intentions
should be to grasp the long and short sword and die.

KATO KIYOMASA, *PRECEPTS*

✢ ✢ ✢

The great day has come – it is your first battle. This is the experience all your study, practice and training have been preparing you for. On the battlefield you will either honour or dishonour your ancestors. Here you will walk away proudly clutching the severed head of a noble enemy – or have your own corpse carried off, having left your noble head behind as a prized trophy. Here will be horrors unmentionable, which Buddhist scholars have likened to the Realm of the Beasts (the level of existence only one layer above Hell itself in the great hierarchy of being through which we pass). Yet here too is glory. Here your destiny will be realized.

Departing for War

Long before the enemy are sighted you will have carried out a great deal of preparation associated with the process of going off to war. This stage must never be neglected, for on it victory will often depend. We have already covered your training, your leadership experience and even your religious beliefs, so we must now turn to the arrangements made immediately prior to departure to avoid bad luck, because it is absolutely vital to ensure that the gods and Buddhas are on your side.

The battlefield is one area where the gods interact with men, so it is vital a samurai honours the gods and prays to them for a victory.

- - - - - - - - - - - - - -

We will assume that before the actual conflict you will have honoured your ancestors, revered the gods of the locality and been well disposed towards your family's Buddhist temple. But you will still need all the help you can get, because the battlefield is the arena where the gods interact with men like nowhere else. Consider the first shogun, Minamoto Yoritomo. He was a fine samurai indeed, but he was also a very pious man and the gods smiled on him in consequence. Not once did he fail to wear religious amulets about his person, and not once did he fail to have sutras (scriptures) chanted by pious monks. Within his closest entourage were priests whose skills allowed them to divine lucky and unlucky days on which to go to war. On the day identified by the principles of yin and yang as the best for going into battle, Minamoto Yoritomo would enact with minute precision all the necessary rituals that would ensure the gods were fighting for him, and not for his enemies the Taira. The latter had disgraced the gods and Buddhas by their overweening pride and therefore deserved chastisement. Yoritomo's pious conduct is an example to us all.

Before any samurai leaves for battle he will wish to eat a farewell meal, a repast that could well prove to be the last he will eat before entering the White Jade Pavilion as a Guest. He will be served dried chestnuts, seaweed and abalone, and will drink a farewell cup of sake. I remember many a similar farewell draught being shared by my old comrades before they went into battle at Imafuku during the winter campaign at Osaka, only a few months ago.

- -

Reliable and efficient food supplies are essential if an army is to be kept in fighting trim. Some provisions will be carried; others may have to be foraged for, or even looted.

When all is complete, the departing general will receive a shout from his men and will mount his horse, ready to ride in splendour out of his castle gates with the serried ranks of his samurai behind him. Great banners will be unfurled, the huge battle standards will be lifted high and the host will depart – though it may be at this crucial moment that the gods appear to show their displeasure. This very serious matter can cause a drop in morale; however, there are ways to overcome the problem, and indeed methods of avoiding it in the first place that go far beyond the veneration of the gods and Buddhas. You begin by divining precisely how lucky the day is, while any bad luck can be avoided by taking such simple precautions as avoiding sexual intercourse the night before, wearing the correct clothes according to the season and shunning any impurity such as menstrual blood or pregnant women. Divination according to the yin and the yang of the particular day must be rigorously applied to the strategic process. To give two simple examples: a samurai born in the Year of the Tiger, when that coincides with the Junior Brother of the Fire, should avoid going to war on Water-Positive Dragon days; while a samurai born on a Fire-Positive Dog day will prosper if he goes to war during any year that is Elder Brother of the Earth (unless it is also a Year of the Rat, in which case he will succeed only if a battle is fought during the Month of Nature's Awakening). It is as straightforward as that.

Indications of divine offence may be shown at the moment of departure by the gods making the lord fall off his horse, drop his bow or some similarly regrettable mishap. Fortunately, at the hands of skilled priests, a divination may be quickly undertaken, revealing that what may appear to ignorant persons as a bad omen is in fact a good omen. So if, for example, the lord's horse bolts and throws him to the ground, it could be interpreted as the will of the gods that the lord should ride into battle very quickly to chastise his enemies. Once this wise interpretation is explained to the army they will fully understand the true nature of the omen.

On the March

The army will now have a long journey ahead of it. Preceding the main body of men will be the scouts; often these will be the elite Courier Guards in their fine horo cloaks. They will continually leave the army and then return to it, keeping the commander up to date about the territory through which they are marching. The main force will move in manageable units, and the most splendid unit of all will be composed of the lord himself, attended by his Horse Guards, his Foot Guards and the rest of his hatamoto with their own personal attendants. Finely dressed samurai will ride or march along, followed by forbidding-looking squads of gunners and spearmen. It is indeed a magnificent sight, but bringing up the rear of this illustrious host will be the necessary baggage train of packhorses, bearers and even ox-drawn carts. Now I get really annoyed when someone tells me that to be put in charge of the baggage train, or to be given any post concerning mundane matters such as food is demeaning, boring or both. This is not so.

Food supplies have to be organized in two ways: the first concerns the stores that you will take with you; the second concerns what can be obtained along the way. For the former you will have a draft unit consisting of horses and labourers. A ten-day supply of food and fodder is not an unreasonable amount to take, and labourers can carry quite heavy weights if you threaten to flog them. Regarding food found along the way, you will have had to organize a system of foraging and a means of cash payment, both of which are based on good intelligence about what lies on the route you plan to take. Looting is acceptable within only enemy territory, and even then it should be carried out with extreme care, because there is more than a slight possibility that the farmers on your enemy's land, squeezed by his outrageous rates of tax and downtrodden by his cruelty, will respond to your example of generosity and goodwill by joining your side instead. To alienate them by looting their crops would be a grave error of judgment.

Should looting from the enemy prove necessary then make sure you pillage properly. There is nothing more annoying than samurai who don't know how to loot effectively, and end up being fooled by enemy farmers who have hidden their supplies in devious ways (such as burying rice bales underground). If you suspect this has happened then seize a peasant, hang him up by his ankles and beat him. In extreme cases, your enemy may have ordered a scorched-earth policy, and there really is nothing to be had. It is therefore wise to keep some provisions in hand. Remember also that water supplies may have been poisoned or simply contaminated with faeces etc. This is an unspeakable crime but it can happen.

I hope this has convinced you that being in charge of the commissariat is an honourable position. Marching at the rear of the column will still give you the chance to earn glory and collect heads. Take, for example, what happened to Uesugi Kenshin in 1561 when his baggage train got cut off from the rest of the army and was then attacked. The general in charge of the stores fought a brave battle, earning himself much honour.

Here we see ashigaru (foot soldiers) carrying bales of rice. Normally this will be done by bearers drafted into an army: a large proportion of an army's manpower consists of people who are there just to carry things.

The Deployment of Samurai on a Battlefield

The enemy are now not very far away, and at this stage everything changes. It is no easy task to convert a marching column of men into battlefield dispositions, but we are indeed fortunate to have had bequeathed to us a number of recommended battle formations, originating in the teachings of that great Chinese emperor, Taizong of Tang.

Because of these set moves it is possible to drill an army to manoeuvre smoothly into position. This can, indeed must, be practised in the courtyard of a castle time and time again. When the movements are firmly embedded in the minds of his soldiers, a commander can order 'Take up the position of the Lying Dragon!' or 'Change to the Flying Geese Formation!' and it will all happen fluently.

One essential feature of all these formations is the location adopted by the commander-in-chief. He will take up a position within his glorious host at the place where he has the best view of the action. The maku (field curtains) will be erected to the side and behind him, his hatamoto will surround him and then orders will go out telling the generals to deploy their samurai or weapon squads in accordance with his wishes.

Let battle commence!

The commander-in-chief sits on a camp-stool in a position where he has a good view of the action. This general is holding a tasselled signalling fan, called a saihai.

Avoid Those Irksome Communications Problems by Good Signalling

The chain of command, in which you will play a varied but vital part, is completely dependent upon good communications. Let us look at what the communication methods are and how they work, because the meticulous ordering of troops I have just described will avail you nothing if one group cannot communicate with another.

1 Visual Signals

The most immediate form of visual communication from a commander to his generals, and thereby to his troops, is made by the waving of his war fan, which he uses as his baton of command. There are three types: the first is the saihai, which is a bundle of paper tassels hung from a baton; the second is exactly like a typical opening fan, but is made of stout iron spines; and the third is a solid wooden fan. With these a general may even defend himself. This happened during the fourth battle of Kawanakajima in 1561: Takeda Shingen was suddenly attacked within his own field curtains and had nothing but his fan with which to defend himself. Seven sword-blows rained down on him from his assailant, who is believed to have been the great Uesugi Kenshin himself.

The commander's fan is the first stage in the signalling process. Here a general rises from his camp-stool to indicate an order with his war fan.

The lowering of a war fan can be seen only at close quarters, so for transmitting an order over larger distances a system of signalling flags is used. Hundreds of ashigaru in any army will have charge of these flags, which are raised or lowered in blocks of at least 12 men, so that a clear signal is given. For example, one block lowered and two blocks vertical could mean 'Advance'. The unit commanders will be looking out for these signals and will respond accordingly.

2 Audible Signals

There are three methods for giving audible signals. The first is to strike the war drums, the deep sounds of which carry far and stir the spirit. There are set drumbeats to indicate advance or retreat, and, unlike any other audible signal, the beat can be increased to enhance the warriors' speed and fighting spirit. The conch shell trumpet (horagai) is another very useful instrument. Its long, mournful sound carries a great distance and is a particularly useful means of communication in mountainous territory, where its non-military use has long been associated with the wandering yamabushi. These mountain ascetics are the best players of the horagai, so try and recruit one into your army; you will not be disappointed. A gong or bell is difficult to discern over the noise of the battlefield, and so these are best confined to timekeeping and ordering life around a camp.

The horagai (conch shell trumpet) is a very useful means of communication on the battlefield. The yamabushi (mountain ascetics) are particularly good at playing the horagai.

3 Personal Signals

Sometimes one cannot risk communicating a message solely by drums or flags. This is where the Courier Guards are so valuable, because they will gallop between allies or different units of the army, conveying messages that are spoken or occasionally written. Theirs is a perilous profession, because crackshots within the enemy army will seek to shoot dead a Courier Guard to hamper the flow of communication.

How Battles Have Changed in the Past Thousand Years

I am sure you will have carefully prepared for your first battle by reading improving literature (some helpful suggestions appear earlier in this book), but it is also important you appreciate that the nature of Japanese warfare has changed over the past thousand years – many of these transformations coming from advances in military technology. A samurai from the Gempei War (1180–85), adept at kyuba no michi (the Way of Horse and Bow), would be lost when faced with a modern arquebus squad. The spirit of the samurai remains unchanged: it is still noble to charge into battle regardless of the consequences, to seek out a noble opponent and earn great personal glory; but many other elements are very different and you need to know about them.

During the Nara period (710–94) it was expected that ordinary people would be drafted into the imperial army, but with the rise of the samurai everything changed. From that time onwards the emphasis was on noble skills with horse and bow; that is until the Mongols taught us a few lessons three centuries ago. They shot volleys of arrows at us and advanced in dense formations. Fortunately, the numerous Japanese civil wars that followed were fought on a suitably man-to-man basis, but the introduction of firearms has made our warfare regress into something like the Mongol tactical method. This is of course regrettable, but the Way of the Warrior requires us to serve our lords however we can, even if this means some diminution in personal glory. When opportunity arises, reward will follow. At the battle of Shizugatake, for example, Lord Toyotomi Hideyoshi named the samurai who fought most valiantly that day as the 'Seven Spears'. To be first into battle remains the greatest obsession for many samurai, and no honour is comparable to it. To be recorded as the warrior who took the first head; as the warrior who took the most heads; as the warrior who took the finest head; or even as the warrior who left the finest head behind on his own corpse provides considerable compensation for the increased anonymity of the modern battlefield. There is also the honour attached to being the first to have killed an enemy using a sword; the first to have done so using a spear and so on. Personally, I really look forward to the day when equal honour will be paid to the samurai who has calmly led others into battle, has controlled their movements successfully, and has returned to serve another day.

Eight Great Battles and What We Can Learn From Them

The most valuable lessons of all come from the battles of the past. Let us take a look at eight notable examples:

1 The Battle of Uji, 1180

As I noted in chapter 1, the reprehensible Taira Kiyomori had married his daughter into the imperial family and had come to dominate the government. In 1180 the Minamoto challenged him, with Minamoto Yorimasa raising a revolt within the monastery of Miidera, his meagre force supplemented by warrior monks. When the Taira advanced against them, Yorimasa and his troops withdrew to the south and made a stand at the bridge across the river at Uji. A long section of planking from the bridge was torn up and the Minamoto awaited a dawn attack. Many deeds of heroism were performed on the broken bridge until the Taira succeeded in crossing by swimming their horses over the river. The situation growing more desperate, Yorimasa withdrew to the nearby temple of Byodo-In, where his sons held off the enemy. He then committed seppuku (ritual suicide) after writing a farewell poem on his war fan, an act that may be regarded as an example to us all. This battle shows heroism on both sides, in both a stubborn defence and a brilliant attack.

Here we see a brave samurai swimming his horse across a river.
This is how the attack was launched at the battle of Uji in 1180,
when the Taira defeated the Minamoto.

2 The Battle of Kawagoe, 1545

In 1545 Ogigayatsu Uesugi together with Ashikaga Haruuji marched against Kawagoe Castle, which was defended by Hojo Ujiyasu's brother Hojo Tsunanari. Tsunanari's garrison was only 3,000 strong, but managed to hold out against 85,000 besiegers. Hojo Ujiyasu marched to Kawagoe's relief with 8,000 samurai, and one brave warrior managed to slip through the Uesugi siege lines to tell Tsunanari that they were on their way. The relief force was another pitifully small army, but intelligence suggested that the besiegers were so confident of victory that their vigilance had slackened. Ujiyasu decided to make a night attack, which was to be coordinated with a sortie from the castle by his brother. Ujiyasu issued orders that his men should not overburden themselves by wearing heavy armour, and should wear white paper jackets to be seen in the dark. He also ordered that they should not waste time by taking heads. It says a lot for the loyalty of the Hojo samurai that they willingly suspended this most basic of samurai privileges for the common good. The plans worked perfectly and, though outnumbered ten to one, the Hojo triumphed. Kawagoe shows us that a night attack can work, but that it has to be coordinated and firmly disciplined.

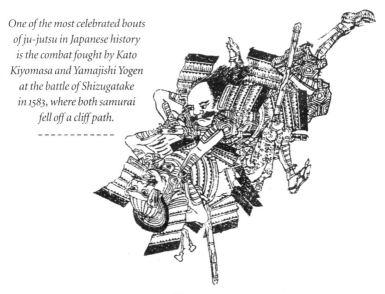

One of the most celebrated bouts of ju-jutsu in Japanese history is the combat fought by Kato Kiyomasa and Yamajishi Yogen at the battle of Shizugatake in 1583, where both samurai fell off a cliff path.

3 The Battle of Okehazama, 1560

This was the first great victory won by Oda Nobunaga, and though no one would wish to denigrate his achievement in any way, it was the behaviour of his opponent Imagawa Yoshimoto that provides the best example in Japanese history of what not to do. Yoshimoto was the first of the great lords of the Age of Warring States to attempt a march on Kyoto to seize the person of the shogun and bend him to his will. His route, along the Tokaido Road, took him through the province of Owari. At first all went well, largely owing to the bravery of His Most Illustrious Highness, who as a youth was made to fight for Lord Imagawa (then his overlord). Having captured the local castle, Yoshimoto set up camp at Okehazama and began a head-viewing ceremony. So engrossed did he become that he did not notice Oda Nobunaga had circled round behind him. The resulting battle lasted about five minutes. Lord Imagawa lost his head, Nobunaga became very famous, and His Most Illustrious Highness was freed from his obligation to fight for a lord who was clearly stupid. Let this be a lesson to us all. Okehazama shows us that a good general must always maintain vigilance.

A messenger brings the news of Nobunaga's attack to an astonished Imagawa Yoshimoto as he sits in state to view the heads after his recent victory. Very soon Yoshimoto was to be killed.

4 The Fourth Battle of Kawanakajima, 1561

The fourth battle of Kawanakajima was the largest of the five encounters between Uesugi Kenshin and Takeda Shingen. Kenshin established a camp high on the hill of Saijoyama, from where he could observe the Takeda movements around Kaizu Castle. Yamamoto Kansuke, Shingen's chief strategist, suggested a clever move: under cover of darkness the Takeda should leave their castle and take up a prearranged position across the river. A detachment would then attack Saijoyama to the rear, driving the Uesugi samurai in panic down the hill, across the river and into the waiting guns of the Takeda army. But Uesugi Kenshin anticipated the operation and evacuated Saijoyama without the Takeda realizing. In great secrecy he guided his army over a ford and positioned them across the river to meet the Takeda. As dawn broke he attacked the Takeda from the flank. According to legend, Shingen and Kenshin fought a single combat when Kenshin broke into the Takeda field headquarters. By this time the detached force sent up from Kaizu Castle had discovered that Saijoyama had been abandoned. Highly alarmed, they came hurrying down to the river, where they encountered Kenshin's rearguard. Fierce fighting continued, and taking full responsibility for the presumed disaster Yamamoto Kansuke committed suicide. But then the Takeda rallied and the Uesugi were driven away. Both sides claimed the victory, which was an expensive one.

This celebrated battle is an object lesson in army control. Both commanders moved huge bodies of troops under cover of darkness and used the set battle formations perfectly. Their samurai then fought to the death.

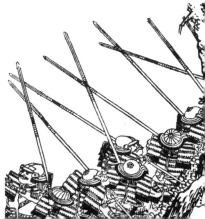

A unit of samurai spearmen going into battle. Organized groups of samurai armed with spears as a primary weapon are a common sight on battlefields.

----

5 The Battle of Mikata ga Hara, 1572

It may surprise readers to see that I have introduced here one of the few battles ever lost by His Most Illustrious Highness, but there is a good reason for it. The mighty army of Takeda Shingen advanced out of the mountains and bore down upon Hamamatsu Castle. His Most Illustrious Highness advanced to engage him upon the flat plain of Mikata ga Hara to the north of Hamamatsu, and as the snow started to fall a fierce battle took place. Totally outnumbered, the Tokugawa were made to retreat, but it is how His Most Illustrious Highness then conducted himself that makes the encounter so memorable. First he sent a detachment to harass the pursuing Takeda at Saigadake. Second, he ordered Sakai Tadatsugu to beat the great war drum in the gatehouse of Hamamatsu to guide the soldiers home, and also to leave the gates wide open. When the Takeda arrived and saw the gates open they feared a trap and withdrew. Note how such ingenuity can triumph against overwhelming odds.

- -

This is a splendid illustration of mounted combat between two samurai with long straight spears. Similar contests occurred at the battles of Kawanakajima and Anegawa.

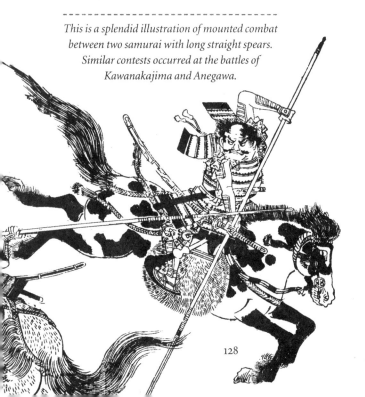

6 The Battle of Nagashino, 1575

This famous battle has frequently been misunderstood. The Takeda army that laid siege to Nagashino Castle were outnumbered by the combined Oda–Tokugawa force of 38,000, who advanced to relieve the siege, setting up positions that looked across the plain of Shidarahara towards the castle. Oda Nobunaga also had the advantage of a unit of 3,000 arquebusiers, but realized that they would need some form of physical protection, so his army built a palisade between the forested edge of the hills and the river. It was a loose fence of stakes, staggered over three alternate layers, and with many gaps to allow a counter-attack. Nobunaga's plan was for the arquebus unit to fire volleys as the Takeda cavalry approached. This broke the charge, but the battle continued until mid-afternoon, when the Takeda eventually began to retreat and were pursued. Some people say Nagashino was a victory for the guns. It was not. It was a victory for common sense in combining and coordinating your forces. Take heed.

7 The Battle of Hetsugigawa, 1586

Hetsugigawa was such a disaster that every young samurai will profit greatly from learning about it. Hideyoshi's vanguard divisions for the invasion of Kyushu were under the command of Chosokabe Motochika and Sengoku Hidehisa, who landed on Kyushu with orders to act defensively until further troops were able to join them. Alas! They decided to disobey Hideyoshi's commands and relieve the castle of Toshimitsu, which was encircled by the Shimazu. The besieging Shimazu army noted their approach and redoubled their efforts to take Toshimitsu, which consequently fell to the rapid and ferocious attack. When the invaders arrived at the Hetsugigawa River, which flowed within sight of the castle, they could see the flags of the Shimazu flying from its towers.

Chosokabe Motochika, the wiser of the leaders, proposed a withdrawal, but his companions insisted on doing battle, so the Shimazu set a trap. Ijuin Hisanori led a decoy force in an attack across the river and then withdrew, which persuaded the left wing of the invading force to follow them. They were met by arrows and arquebus fire, and the main body of the Shimazu then fell upon them. After much fierce fighting the left wing withdrew across the river, causing confusion within the right wing. Chosokabe Motochika was obliged to signal a full retreat, during which his son and heir Nobuchika was killed. This is what happens when you disobey orders!

8 The Battle of Sacheon, 1598

This was one of the last battles of our glorious second expedition to Korea. The castle of Sacheon held a garrison of 8,000 troops under the father-and-son team of Shimazu Yoshihiro and Tadatsune (now Lord Shimazu Iehisa). By the middle of September 1598 the Chinese General Ton Yuan had assembled an army of 34,000 Chinese troops together with 2,000 Koreans, and on 1 October 1598 this allied army arrived at Sacheon – just too late to stop our reinforcements joining Shimazu Yoshihiro in the castle. Both sides used great ingenuity in their attack and defence. The Chinese brought up a combined battering ram and cannon against the main gate; we managed to destroy it, and also launched exploding firebombs by catapult into the midst of the Chinese army, with one shot hitting the Chinese gunpowder store. On the last day of the siege, Shimazu Yoshihiro took the initiative and led his army out to meet the Chinese and Koreans in a field battle. The force of our attack broke the besieging army, who were driven back as far as the river with many casualties. Here we see an example of desperate defence being turned into a successful attack.

Here we see a group of samurai committing suicide on the battlefield. Such an act is an excellent way of retaining one's honour when defeat is inevitable.

Frequently Asked Questions about Battlefield Etiquette

You are now poised to engage your enemy with your sword drawn, eager to take his head. All you are waiting for is the command to advance. What thoughts are now passing through your mind? Let's deal with some frequently asked questions concerning this precise scenario and the immediate events that may have preceded it.

Q Should I have slaughtered my wife and children before leaving for battle?

A This is rarely necessary. There have been occasions when a lord, departing for what he believes will be his last battle and fearful of the consequences that will befall his family in the event of his death, decides to kill all of them just to be on the safe side. But this is by no means a universal recommendation.

Q Should I have perfumed my hair?

A Yes, oh yes. This will make your head so much more attractive when it is cut off.

Q Should I play dead and then attempt to murder the victorious enemy general?

A This was tried by Akechi Mitsuchika, who concealed himself among the dead bodies at Yamazaki in 1582 and then rose up to kill Hideyoshi. It was commendable. You must decide for yourself if it is appropriate under the given circumstances.

Q I have heard it said that challenges to individual combat are out of date. Is this in fact the case?

A Throughout samurai history there has never been a more honourable way of fighting than to conduct a single combat with a worthy opponent. There is certainly less opportunity nowadays, largely owing to the vastly increased size of the typical samurai army and the use of mass-infantry tactics. Nevertheless, in the confusion of battle you may well find yourself on your own with a choice of opponent. The family crest on his flag will confirm his allegiance, but there is no way of ascertaining his personal status (and so whether he is a worthy victim) other than by inviting him to declare his pedigree. He may well be willing to do this, but remember that every second this takes provides a further opportunity for you to be shot dead by an ignoble bullet fired by a lewd and sordid person who would never dare challenge you (let alone invite you to recite your family history). Think carefully.

Q Is it worth collecting the heads of foot soldiers?

A Yes. Many are brave fighters, and the number of heads you collect will be a factor in your eventual reward. Remember, however, the example of the Hojo at Kawagoe; head collecting takes time. Might you be better employed cutting off more heads, rather than collecting the ones you already have?

Q My lord has ordered me to burn down a shrine. I am afraid of causing offence to the gods. Should I obey orders?

A This is a very tricky question. Of course you should obey orders, but where is the lord who would wish to burn down a shrine? Decades ago this was common practice among the lords who misguidedly accepted as true the lies and deceits of Christianity. They were all chastised for it, and received the punishment of Heaven. I am sure this appalling dilemma will never arise nowadays.

Q My lord has ordered me to perform an act of incredible bravery from which I will not return alive. What should I do?

A Do you really not know the answer to this question?

Q I suspect the sentry next to me of being a ninja on account of his unusual behaviour. Should I kill him?

A No. He may just be having a bad day. Have him arrested and beaten; that way the truth will emerge.

ℚ I have been placed in command of a unit of ronin. The enemy have charged us and the ronin have all run away. Should I join them?

🅐 No, you are a true samurai; they are not. You must not blame yourself for errors in personnel recruitment that have their origins higher up the chain of command. Stand your ground and die bravely.

ℚ A fellow samurai has offered me a severed head, saying I can claim it as my own trophy if I hand over money to him. Should I accept?

🅐 Certainly not. Such a worthless fellow is the very dregs of the sake barrel of life. He is probably such a rascal that the head will previously have belonged to some poor farmer that he has cut down. How reprehensible!

ℚ I am totally surrounded by enemies. My helmet is off my head, my suit of armour looks like a porcupine due to the number of arrows sticking into it and my sword is broken. What should I do now?

🅐 Turn quickly to the section headed 'Fourteen Interesting Ways to Commit Suicide' in chapter 12.

What is Going On Behind the Smoke?

Your unit has been moved into position, has been ordered forwards and subsequently engaged the enemy. You have now reached the most important stage in the development of a battle – contact has been made. This is truly the Realm of the Beasts! All around you are the sounds of swords striking armour, of horses whinnying and guns being discharged, while terrible screams and loud shouts add to the cacophony of noise. War has been much like this for centuries, but because of arquebuses the modern battlefield is an even more noisy and confusing place than it has been at any other time in history. I have outlined above some of what occurs prior to battle, but what actually happens when two armies clash? Communications break down, orders are forgotten and all is confusion – a situation made worse by the smoke produced by thousands of arquebuses. The battle has probably developed into a melee where one samurai hacks at another, oblivious of everything other than what is happening a spear's length around him. Can you find a worthy opponent to challenge? Can you even see him amid the smoke? Have you been assaulted instead by six ashigaru spearmen who are trying to pin you down with their blades like a trapped animal? First your spear breaks, then your sword is lost; soon your dagger too falls from your grasp. Essentially, you are on your own – exactly the situation that the whole of this book thus far has been preparing you for. You are a true samurai, so may the gods be with you!

Fighting Techniques for the Noble Samurai

Let us assume that you have been taught the bugei (techniques of martial arts) by an accomplished sensei, and have taken every opportunity to practise them. This will have happened within the walls of your castle or on the hunting field. You now have to put these techniques into operation … with one very important difference. Unlike every previous encounter, the man you are fighting wants to kill you.

Archery from Horseback

Let us first deal with fighting while mounted. This will normally take one of two forms: the samurai acting as either a horse archer or a spearman. The former is encountered less often nowadays, and the most important point to be made is that you will not be acting as a light horse archer. These warriors from Mongolia that we sometimes read about can behave almost like acrobats, swinging round in the saddle, discharging arrows as they retreat and so on. You, by contrast, will be wearing a heavier suit of armour, greatly restricting your movements. The most noticeable constraint upon your physical freedom will be the limitation of being able to shoot effectively only to the left. Loosing arrows ahead of you is just about possible, but it will be very difficult indeed to twist your body in the saddle sufficiently to release arrows to the right (assuming you are right handed). Your opponent will be suffering the same limitations. This also means that when firing an arrow at an individual or a group you will be exposing a great deal of yourself as a target. It is here that the techniques of the martial art of yabusame, which allows you to discharge an arrow to your left side with accuracy and at speed, will serve you well. Note also that you will withdraw your arrows from the quiver located on your right side, so practice in smoothly fitting the nock to the string and drawing the bow while you stay in perfect balance is absolutely essential.

Spear-fighting from Horseback

Using a spear successfully from horseback is quite a different matter, and will depend on whether you are acting as an individual warrior or as part of a group. A group will tend to be ordered into a coordinated charge, and in this case it is best for the spear to be held rigidly with the blade pointing forwards so you can skewer your opponent like a wild boar. The forwards movement of the horse will provide an impact that your arms could never supply. When used like this in Europe the spear is, I believe, referred to as a 'lance'. This technique is much more difficult when used against another mounted opponent, who will be trying to impale you on his own spear at the same time. Try to receive his blow against an area of your armour that has a smooth surface so that it glances off, while directing your spear against a more vulnerable part of his armour.

The close formation demanded by a unit's charge rules out any freer use of the spear, lest you hurt one of your comrades; however, when you are on your own the spear may be wielded far more liberally. Instead of just thrusting, you can stand in the stirrups holding the spear in both hands, sweeping it to the sides as a slashing and cutting weapon, rather than just a stabbing arm. This is where longer-bladed spears are the best, and kamayari (cross-bladed spears) allow the possibility of pulling a foot soldier off his feet, or dragging a horseman from his saddle. Kato Kiyomasa was famous for his expertise with a long-bladed spear (with one short cross blade), which he employed very effectively. The ultimate slashing weapon to use from the saddle is the naginata with its long curved blade, but as its balance is totally different this must be regarded as a specialist weapon like the heavy and unwieldy nodachi (extra-long sword). Both are best left to experts, as I noted earlier.

Pistol techniques from Horseback

I am given to understand that a whole new set of techniques is being developed for the use of handguns from the saddle. It is envisaged that, in addition to the pistol being used as an individual weapon, organized groups of mounted samurai will gallop up to the enemy lines and discharge their weapons. The resulting casualties among the enemy ranks will disorganize them, at which the attacking force will discard their pistols and draw their swords for a melee, riding into the gaps left in the enemy formation.

Sword-fighting from Horseback

Using swords from horseback will be required if spears or bows have to be discarded, and the fighting techniques used need to be very free and open. To strike downwards from a moving horse adds a tremendous extra force to the power of a sword-cut, so much so that armour plates and helmets are known to have been sliced in two. As the horse gallops forwards, the sword-blade is dragged deeper into the wound, severing limbs and heads with great rapidity. Sword combat between two mounted samurai is an awesome sight: the warriors slash at each other with weapons held in one hand while clutching the reins with the other.

The spirit of the samurai is perfectly exemplified by this bronze statue of Nasu Shingo (1829–63) at Yusuhara on Shikoku Island. He was one of the companions of Sakamoto Ryoma, a prominent loyalist in the wars of the Meiji Restoration through which Japan entered the modern world.

The death of Wani Chikazane at the siege of Tanaka Castle in 1587 is re-enacted as part of the annual Sengoku Higo Kunishu Matsuri (a festival that commemorates the disastrous rebellion of the minor lords of Higo province in 1587) in February 2011, Nagomi town, Kumamoto prefecture. Tanaka was one of the centres of the rebellion launched against the daimyo Sassa Narimasa.

The firing of an arquebus by a member of the Marugame Teppo-kai, the musketry re-enactment group of Marugama City, where this demonstration is taking place The arquebus, which revolutionized Japanese warfare, was similar to a simple matchlock musket.

Yabusame (mounted archery) is here performed at the Nikko Toshogu Shrine during the spring festival in 2008. The riders have to shoot three arrows against wooden targets set along the track. Yabusame essentially derives from hunting rather than battle (when arrows tended not to be launched at a gallop).

One of the more unusual martial arts was the technique of swimming – and perhaps even operating weapons – while wearing a suit of armour. In this photograph (taken in the Kumamoto prefecture on the island of Kyushu) we see a modern practitioner demonstrating the front crawl while wearing a suit of yoroi-style armour, complete with an iron helmet.

ABOVE *In this suit of armour the colour of the lacing on the breastplate presents the shape of a cross. On the helmet are two kuwagata (antlers).*

PREVIOUS PAGES *The keep of Matsumoto Castle dates back to 1597, making it Japan's oldest surviving tower keep. With its massive stone base and soaring turrets, Matsumoto is one of the finest examples of the developed style of Japanese castle.*

A suit of armour finished with kebiki-odoshi (close-spaced) lacing of white cords and fur trim. On top of the helmet is a crest in the form of a yamabushi's pillbox hat.

A modern reproduction of the ornate horned helmet worn by Yamamoto Kansuke, Takeda Shingen's leading strategist, who committed suicide at the fourth battle of Kawanakajima in 1561 when he saw that his bold plans had brought about an apparent defeat.

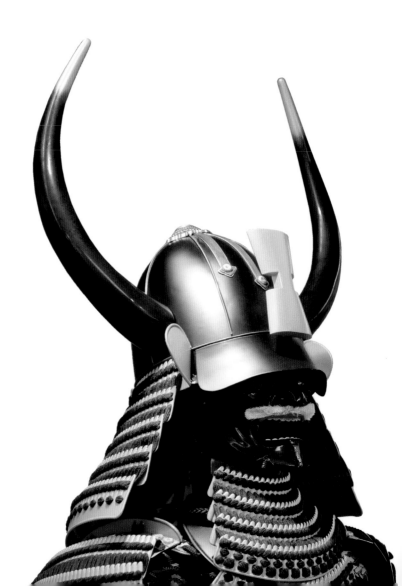

Spear-Fighting Techniques on Foot

It is very unusual for samurai on foot to fight in tightly controlled formations. Instead it has long been recognized that the individual warrior is best employed if he is allowed to make his own decisions about whom he fights. It is quite obvious that he will wish to seek out a noble opponent, but on the modern battlefield this is not always possible: a samurai should never shrink from combat merely because he finds his enemies vulgar. All enemies are potential victims, and all must be overcome if your lord's will is to prevail. So think of yourself as the individual warrior that you have always wanted to be and take the fight to anyone who presents the opportunity. Depending on your rank you will be attended by one or more followers who will hand weapons to you, warn you of dangers and see to it that any combat in which you are fighting is not interrupted by another. Learn to rely on their judgment and you will not suffer the sad fate of Yubu Oinosuke at the siege of Tanaka Castle in 1587. This gallant warrior ran forwards to engage an enemy, but his attendants realized that it was an ambush and called him back. Poor Yubu was practically deaf, did not hear their warnings, and so perished. Let this not be your fate also.

Spear-fighting on foot involves using the weapon both for attack and defence. A spear's protective role is best demonstrated when it knocks to one side the attacking blade of an enemy, either with a quick parry or by slowly forcing it down using your own superior strength. You can then follow up with a rapid thrust of your own, which will almost always be more effective than attempting a slashing movement. Aim for the weak points in a suit of armour: the eyes, the throat and the armpits. A thrust delivered directly against the breastplate will probably slide off harmlessly. If, however, your enemy is wearing an old-fashioned suit of armour with close-spaced cord lacing then the blade may catch in and penetrate the cords, but again the plates beneath will probably prevent any injury.

The great advantage of a spear over a sword is that it keeps your opponent at a safe distance. Yes, you can seize the shaft or even cut through it, as Imagawa Yoshimoto did at the battle of Okehazama, but this is difficult to achieve and leaves you open to a quick and opportunistic sword-stroke. Think of a spear as an extension of your arm; the greatest means of defence is maintaining the gap between you and an opponent, and the greatest chance of achieving a kill lies in your ability to fill that gap very quickly.

Sword Combat on Foot

Two samurai face each other on the battlefield with their swords drawn; is this not the ideal to which we all aspire? Indeed it is, but we must recognize that most sword combat on foot takes place within a disorganized melee, where a samurai may have to take on two or three opponents at once, all the while beset by arrows and bullets discharged by distant warriors. This will be a contest marked by near-random hacking against anyone wearing a different flag from that of your own lord. You will cut with your sword as if creating space within a dense bed of reeds. Here only the strongest will prevail, and this involves strength of character as much as physical prowess because the samurai must be alert to any development and must not relax his guard even for one moment. The samurai who pauses in a melee to pick up an attractively helmeted head as a trophy will soon become a trophy himself.

In the happy instances when a samurai can devote himself to just one opponent, the skills of both men may be exercised as if they were in the courtyard of their respective lords' castles. If the pair are known to be great warriors then those around them will almost certainly allow them the luxury of uninterrupted combat. Their attendants will not fight against one another but will act as seconds: holding their master's sashimono (as these back flags are an encumbrance in single combat); standing ready with a spare spear or sword; or simply acting as witnesses to the great deed of arms that will be sung about for centuries to come. Unlike encounters within the melee, single combats allow the fighters to take their time and adopt a guard position, because they both know that danger can come from only one direction. So they eye each other up, and when their weapons clash they do so with a force and impact greater even than the fierce blows that they once delivered with their practice wooden swords. The swords are now of steel and the target is a body encased in armour. As blows begin to fall, the cords holding sections of armour together will be the first to perish, so that the two warriors will soon present a sorry appearance – their shoulder plates and skirt sections hanging in tatters, chips cut out of the lacquer on their breast-plates. If helmets are lost then the head, with its wild shock of disordered hair, becomes a target. Sooner or later, one will land a blow against a vulnerable section of the armour (such as the groin or the neck) and then the effect of the wounds will begin to tell, until the weaker samurai can defend no more. His opponent will then land the final and merciful blow. As the dead man falls the victor will draw his dagger or short-sword and carefully cut off the defeated's head.

No one should interfere in a single combat unless absolutely neces-sary. Even if you have lost sword, spear and dagger, and are now reduced to fighting with bare hands, you must still expect to be solely responsible for the eventual outcome. So grapple with your opponent, try with all your might to force him off balance and throw him to the ground. You can then apply a ju-jutsu hold that will immobilize him – the wrist is a very good target for this. Alternatively you can put him in a hold using the weight of your body on top, or even strangle him. When the man falls silent and goes limp you can cut off his head.

10
Castles and Sieges – A Very Different Challenge

I sincerely assure you that of all the palaces and houses I have seen in Portugal, India and Japan, there has been nothing to compare with this.

LUÍS FRÓIS, SJ, ON VISITING GIFU CASTLE

The open field of battle is the arena where every samurai prefers to demonstrate his skills, but, like it or not, the majority of actions in which you take part will probably involve a fortified place. This provides new challenges and calls for an entirely different set of skills, but it also allows for the acquisition of considerable glory in an often-difficult situation.

Castles, which are fantastic creations of white wood and blue tiles, ornamented with gold, soar above great stone walls like exquisitely decorated samurai helmets. Yet castles were not always like this. For years most castles were built entirely from wood, producing temporary and flimsy structures. These early yamashiro (mountain castles) consisted of a complex of interlocking defensive spaces, carved from the tops of adjacent hills and mountains, with a lord's living quarters positioned in a valley. Castle walls were the existing wooded hillsides, while their towers were built from the wood of trees removed both to provide building space and to ensure a clear field of view. As time went by, lords created numerous distant mountain-top outposts that were controlled from one central castle; and it was not long before certain imaginative lords developed the most distinctive feature of our Japanese castles: the massive stone bases on which a more elaborate superstructure can sit. Thousands of workmen clear the vegetation from a hillside, then follow a precise geometric pattern to clad the slopes in stone. As well as being a defensive feature, the solidity of the base also provides good protection from earthquakes. No mortar is used in the building of the substructure, and at first sight it looks as if the stones of the walls have been placed haphazardly, but in fact they are carefully arranged with their smaller sides outwards and their larger sides inwards, resulting in a fine concave curve. Kumamoto Castle, the seat of Lord Kato Kiyomasa, provides an excellent example of this. Above these bases may be seen another form of wall, which is a low construction of plaster over a wood and rope core that runs along the length of the stone base defence. These walls are tiled as a protection against rain, and are pierced with loopholes for guns and bows. Every castle has several gateways, with the gatehouses hung with doors of heavy timber on massive iron hinges, reinforced with iron plates and spikes.

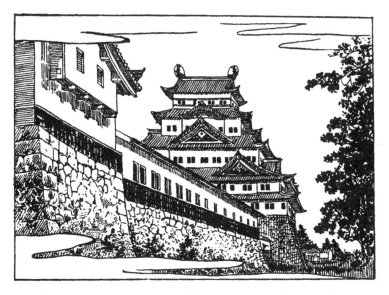

The keep of Nagoya Castle – one of the finest examples of the magnificent fortifications that grace the landscape of Japan – acts as a defensive and administrative centre for the domains of a daimyo.

The earlier model of a lord's living quarters lying in a valley connected to a lookout tower on a nearby hill has long since been replaced by one massive complex, where the hill itself has disappeared under a maze of intersecting stone bases, towers, walkways, parapets and gatehouses, crowned by a splendid many-floored keep that allows a commanding view of the lord's territory and provides a crucial symbol of his power. More mundanely, it also provides a solid last-ditch refuge in times of war, should every other tower and courtyard of the castle have fallen to an enemy. This is precisely the situation faced by those misguided rebels at Osaka.

Regardless of its military function, the keep of a modern castle is also a truly beautiful sight. The windows, roofs and gables are arranged in subtle and intricate patterns, with the roofs almost always tiled – the topmost ridge decorated with ornaments in the shape of fish as charms against evil spirits and fire. The external colour of keeps is usually white, but exceptions are the so-called 'black castles', such as Kumamoto, Matsue and Okayama. Here the darker predominant colour comes from the black wood, which is more pervasive than the surrounding white plaster. The family crest of the lord carved on the apex of the gable ends is the only other decoration. A Japanese castle is therefore both a fortress and a thing of great beauty.

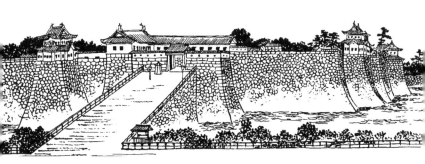

The outer wall and moat of Osaka Castle, built by Toyotomi Hideyoshi in 1586.

How Castles Fail – Ten Things Every Castle Owner Should Know

Let us look at how these beautiful castles are defended. Unfortunately many incorrect preconceptions still exist, which I shall deal with here:

1 Castles are still made mostly out of wood

Centuries ago castles were entirely wooden structures, but even today, with the development of stone bases, enough of a castle is built from wood to make fire your greatest enemy. Don't let a lazy cook undo the work of decades. Fire precautions should always be taken and vigilance maintained at all times.

2 Castle sites are not all the same

Location, location, location! Is your castle a yamashiro (built on a hill) or a hirajiro (built on a plain)? Does it defend a port or an estuary? Is it accessed by land or by sea, along narrow mountain paths or across rice fields? All these are important factors that must be taken into consideration when defending or attacking a fortified place.

3 Sloping stone walls are better than sheer ones

Japanese castle walls slope quite dramatically, but this does not stop them being relatively easy to climb; so why aren't they built vertically like the Great Wall of China? First, because they are not structurally like Chinese walls: most Japanese stone walls enclose a solid mound of earth, usually sculpted from a mountain, so they naturally slope. Second, because this curved base helps reduce the effects of earthquakes on the structure. If you look at the best-constructed walls, of which, as I have already mentioned, Kumamoto Castle has very good examples, you will notice that even though the fortifications slope they also have quite smooth surfaces, making them tougher to climb. Even if your enemy manages to surmount the stone bases, it doesn't mean that he will be able to enter the keep or the towers. Inside them you will have trapdoors through which you can shoot and drop rocks. Protruding spikes will also hinder an attacker.

4 Castles are not waterproof

The short vertical walls located above the massive stone bases are made of rammed earth and clay. They are plastered and then whitewashed. On top of them runs a roof of shingles or tiles. Neglect the upkeep of this system and one day after heavy rain you will have a soggy mess to clear up. Maintaining the clay mixture on top of the wood is time-consuming and labour-intensive, but ignore it at your peril. Set up a maintenance rota among your farmers so they have something to do on a slack day. If they are needed in the rice fields, get their wives and children to do it.

5 Samurai use cannon

Once we didn't – but we do now. We couldn't have defeated the rebels in the winter campaign of Osaka last year had we not been able to lob a 16-pound shot into the keep, forcing their side to the negotiating table (and smashing the tea cabinet of Toyotomi Hideyori's mother). I may add that the use of cannon is a very recent trend in Japanese warfare. Until we bought English artillery, nothing we had could fire a cannon-ball more than about half a mile. Those Portuguese breech-loaders were hopeless; all the force leaked out round the chamber. Now we have muzzle-loading iron cannon that can hit the keep of Osaka Castle from a safe distance.

6 Some samurai betray castles

How sad this is, but, suppose it is you besieging a castle – if you have a particular defender's wife held hostage and make it clear that she will be crucified in sight of the castle unless he sets fire to the keep, I think he may just be persuaded to abandon several centuries of samurai tradition. This could of course happen to you, so always be on your guard against treason. Have your most trusted samurai posted on the towers just to look out for arrow-letters. These are shot into a castle to seduce weak spirits with offers of riches if they betray you – such letters should be burned immediately. Do not ever open them.

7 You cannot manage without a well

Some people think you can, and collect only rainwater. Try it one day; it's amazing how quickly those storage jars get depleted. Many sieges have ended shortly after the besiegers cut off the water supply. A castle that is dependent upon a nearby stream being piped in, or worst of all relies on water (other than rainfall) being carried up a hill, will not hold out for long. Remember the siege of Chokoji in 1570, where all that Shibata Katsuie had was water stored in jars. In the end he smashed the jars and led his samurai out in a daring, desperate charge.

8 There is not room in your castle for everyone

On this point you will have to be very strict. The more people you pack into the castle, the less food there is to go round: a careful balance must always be struck between augmenting your defensive numbers and not acquiring many useless mouths to feed. It is remarkable, however, how useful some people can be, and peasants don't require much food anyway. Women will fight too, if necessary, as they did during the unusual incident at the siege of Omori Castle in 1600. There the noble samurai of Otani Yoshitsugu found themselves bombarded by stones flung out of the castle from catapults operated by female crews. One samurai was killed. Women and girls can also be set to work casting bullets, repairing damaged armour and of course preparing severed heads for inspection. Even old men can lift quite heavy loads, so set them to work carrying boxes of arrows, bullets and stones up on to the parapets.

9 Your castle will be relieved one day ... won't it?

It may – one day. Let us look at the nightmare situation of not being relieved, such as befell Kikkawa Tsuneie at the siege of Tottori Castle in 1581. Toyotomi Hideyoshi had surrounded the mountain on which the castle was built and erected watchtowers, from which sharpshooters cut down anyone who tried to flee. Kikkawa Tsuneie held out for an amazing 200 days, during which his garrison ate dead horses and even the bodies of deceased comrades. Kato Kiyomasa thought that his end had likewise come in 1593, when he defended Ulsan Castle in Korea for a long and painful time. Eventually he saw flocks of scavenging birds descending on the Chinese siege lines and knew that a Japanese army had arrived. The experience taught him many lessons, and within the vast courtyards of his old castle at Kumamoto there now grow nut trees to provide food in times of siege. Furthermore, all the mats in the building are stuffed not with rice straw as is usual but with dried vegetables, so that a desperate garrison could even eat the floor.

This picture shows the awful conditions that developed during the long siege of Tottori Castle in 1581. The starving defenders are eating a dead horse, and will very soon start eating each other.

----

10 You should worry about ninja

Your castle will not stand for long if you are assassinated. Remember my earlier comments about these despicable villains called ninja and be on your guard.

How to Attack Castles

So much for defending castles; some day you will be called upon to attack one, and they are by no means impregnable. In time even Osaka will fall. All it takes is a little cunning and a lot of bravery, so let us first look at the siegework techniques that are currently employed.

1 Bribery

Why waste valuable samurai when you can buy surrender? It is amazing how often an enemy commander can be persuaded to surrender his castle in return for a handsome bribe of money, lands and titles. If you also threaten to crucify his captured wife, this will concentrate his mind most admirably.

2 Taking By Storm – Everyone's Favourite

When it comes to covering yourself in samurai glory, there is no substitute for an out-and-out assault. Forget all I have just written about castle walls being difficult to climb and just charge. Spears can be awkward in this situation, so hand yours to a personal attendant and clamber up the wall with your sword and dagger. One of those newfangled pistols could also be very useful here. The best tactic to adopt is to order your ashigaru arquebus squads to maintain a continuous rotating volley of fire. This will make the defenders keep their heads down while you and your brave comrades safely cross over the parapet. This was tried first of all by Oda Nobunaga at Muraki in 1564, and was a great success. The archers will augment the process by delivering precisely aimed arrows towards the weapon slits on the castle walls. The best demonstration of this technique was during the first invasion of Korea, where our arquebus troops cleared the walls of Korean defenders at Busan and Jinju.

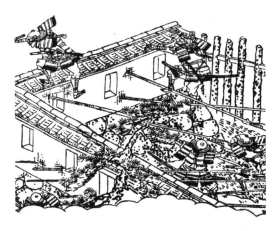

Here we see a spirited attack on a castle wall using spears. The samurai have scaled the massive stone base and are breaking through a short plastered wall pierced with gunports.

- - - - - - - - - - - - - - - - - - -

3 Cannon, Crossbows and Catapults

Any technique whereby missiles may be launched is very useful, but apart from long-range European cannon, large missile weapons such as catapults are more useful for defence than for attack. Siege crossbows were much used in the olden days, but less so now because they are cumbersome and need specialist operators. Siege engines (like the towers and ladders that the Chinese use) are generally also cumbersome, and practical only when a castle is built on a flat plain. As most Japanese castles make use of high ground in some form, they are less susceptible to this kind of attack. The Dutch have recently introduced us to specialized cannon called mortars. They are currently being tested and are very promising because they lob an exploding shell over a castle wall on a high trajectory, causing a greater impact.

4 Exploding Cows and Other Fiendish Chinese Devices

As I mentioned, during the war in Korea our brave samurai were subjected to a wide variety of Chinese siege weapons, but mobile scaling ladders are not the end of the story – far from it! Those clever Chinese have a vast repertoire of bizarre devices in their armoury. Just in case we ever have to fight them again, here are a few details about the Chinese expertise in creating fire. For example, have you ever heard of exploding cows? By this I don't just mean causing cows to stampede by fixing burning brands to their horns (though this can be very effective, as shown by Minamoto Yoshinaka at the battle of Kurikara in 1183 and Hojo Soun at Odawara in 1495). No, rather I refer to the use of one or two animals as delivery systems for explosive devices. The bomb, fitted with a timing fuse, is attached to the animal's rump and the unfortunate beast is driven in the general direction of the target, which is usually a wooden gateway in a castle's walls. The results can be imagined. There is a reliable account of an exploding cow being used in 1132 by the Song defenders at the Chinese city of De'an to destroy the scaling ladders of the Jin dynasty's army. A less dramatic example of the use of expendable animals to spread fire is the employment of birds that have small containers of burning tinder attached to their legs. When the birds settle on the enemy's rooftops, the tinder will set fire to the thatch. I am not sure how the birds distinguish between enemy houses and friendly ones, but don't let's be pedantic.

One of the most surprising Chinese siege techniques involves the use of expendable animals. Here we see a diagram for fitting a bomb to a cow's back.

- - - - - - - - - - -

5 Blockade and Starvation – Two Necessary Evils

A noble samurai is at his best in an active situation, plunging into a moat, clambering up stone walls and engaging in combat along a castle's parapets. But what of those times when he simply has to sit down and wait? It is not easy, as exemplified by Lord Hideyoshi when he made war against His Most Illustrious Highness in 1584. The Tokugawa and the Toyotomi armies had a great respect for each other, having already fought during the famous battle of Nagashino, where the mounted samurai of the Takeda were broken by gunfire delivered from very simple field positions. As a result, when these two giants of warfare confronted each other at Komaki, their first reactions were to build field defences. Boredom inevitably followed, and Lord Hideyoshi, in a display of uncharacteristic impatience, ordered a diversionary frontal attack while his army made a wide circle to attack His Most Illustrious Highness's own province. It was well executed, and His Most Illustrious Highness became aware of the trick only very late in the day. With the generalship for which he is renowned, however, His Most Illustrious Highness went on to defeat Toyotomi Hideyoshi at the battle of Nagakute, the only reverse suffered by Hideyoshi in his entire career. Komaki had come about only because both sides were bored by a stalemate. I relate this story merely to point out to you that sitting down and waiting for surrender can try the patience of even the greatest samurai. To Lord Hideyoshi's credit, there were many other occasions when he was willing to wait, such as at the dreadful siege of Tottori, when the garrison were reduced to cannibalism. Patience is a virtue, young samurai.

Weapon Techniques during Castle Attacks

You will soon discover that the press of a melee during a field battle is nothing compared to the restrictions on movement occasioned by an attack on a castle. Imagine hundreds of samurai trying to climb the stone base of a castle; they will be almost fighting each other for handholds as rocks dropped by the garrison fall around them, some taking men to their deaths in the moat. Once the stone bases are surmounted the white walls have to be climbed, and often the only way to make an entrance is by hacking away the plaster and lath to create a hole. A fight inside the castle courtyard will tend to be a disorganized affray, and then you will be faced with the desperate situation of using spears and swords within the narrow corridors and below the low ceilings of the rooms. Spears have to be used only as thrusting weapons, and even a swung short sword can catch in a lintel and become useless. The stairs inside a keep will be very steep, so that when wounded men fall down, they take their comrades with them. Blinding smoke from arquebus fire soon fills the space, and when a keep is set alight there is no alternative but to leave. If you stay the smoke will fill your lungs and kill you long before the flames do.

Naval Warfare – Pirates or Professionals?

Japan has a long and honourable maritime tradition, although our good name in this regard has recently been besmirched by gangs of pirates who attack Chinese and Korean ships. Many of these ruffians operate from bases on the Goto Islands or from the coastline of Kyushu, so that our overseas neighbours have taken to calling them 'Japanese pirates'. This is both insulting and inaccurate. Most of their leaders are in fact Chinese renegades, and successive shoguns have clearly demonstrated the official attitude to such felons by boiling them alive whenever they are captured. No, if we are to take pride in our sea-fighting expertise let it be due to the glorious navies of our maritime lords.

Fighting at sea is very different from fighting on land. Unlike the sleek Portuguese warships, ours are slow and clumsy, making naval warfare into something very similar to an attack on a castle. When two ships engage there will be an exchange of fire from arquebuses and the throwing of bombs. Men with grappling hooks will then try and secure the ships, after which a sword-fight will take place, accompanied by all the confusion I earlier associated with castles.

If you are a general called upon to go to war at sea, you will be faced with a difficult choice: should you send you own samurai out on to the waves (an environment where they may feel most uncomfortable) or should you entrust the operation to your own professional navy – assuming that you have one? Many lords do neither, tending instead to recruit the services of ex-pirates. Is this wise? Now, in my humble and yet considered opinion there is no such thing as an ex-pirate. Yes, I know that Lord Kuki Yoshitaka, the Admiral of the Fleet to Lord Oda Nobunaga, had something of a dubious background, but he fought well and defeated the Mori fleet at the battle of Kizugawaguchi in 1578. It's just that one really can't trust these people.

11
After the Battle

After the battle, tighten the cords of your helmet.

TOKUGAWA IEYASU, SPEAKING AT
THE BATTLE OF SEKIGAHARA

✥ ✥ ✥

You have won the battle and you have survived. What now? You are tired, thirsty; your hair is dishevelled and you are covered in blood. It is so tempting to throw yourself on the ground and sleep, but you cannot. The most important thing is not to be complacent. Just remember Imagawa Yoshimoto at the battle of Okehazama. Ambushes and counter-attacks can occur at any time, so you must never drop your guard. Lord Oda Nobunaga, it must be said, had the wit to learn from his enemy's mistakes. As he sat within his maku (field curtains) after the battle of Anegawa, one of the Asakura samurai – disguised as one of Nobunaga's own Horse Guards – sneaked into the tent. The man was swiftly spotted by guards, who were tired but still alert, and put to death.

A badly injured samurai on the battlefield tries to raise himself using his sword as the blood flows from his wounds and soaks into the cords of his armour.

What Should We Do with a Defeated Enemy?

Let us demolish once and for all a very common myth about samurai in battle. The popular view is that after an army is defeated there is nothing left of it. The losing side, it is assumed, will be completely eliminated because their samurai have (a) been killed during the fighting, (b) been executed afterwards or (c) committed suicide. Nothing could be further from the truth. A defeated commander may well be expected to suffer death in one of these three ways, but there is no reason why his followers should meet the same fate on a wide scale. There are occasions when massacres are appropriate, such as after defeating the Ikko-ikki or Christians (indeed any despicable and sordid rabble who will never accept samurai rule and must be made to suffer the consequences), but good fighting men of the samurai class are a precious commodity. It was for this reason that at the time of the final defeat of Takeda Katsuyori by His Most Illustrious Highness in 1582, thousands of Takeda samurai became absorbed into the Tokugawa army. The process was greatly helped by the fact that Lord Oda Nobunaga gave his protégé, His Most Illustrious Highness Tokugawa Hidetada, the former Takeda provinces of Kai, Shinano and Suruga as his reward. His Most Illustrious Highness's first move was to dedicate a shrine to the memory of the defeated leader Takeda Katsuyori: a wise gesture that was blessed indeed, causing harmony to prevail. Similarly, when His Most Illustrious Highness assisted Lord Toyotomi Hideyoshi in the capture of the Hojo's Odawara Castle in 1590 he was granted in reward the former Hojo provinces of the Kanto. Of the Hojo leadership none was left, all having committed honourable suicide. Their samurai now serve happily and diligently under the flags of His Most Excellent Highness.

The Head-Viewing Ceremony – Tips from the Experts

I hate to mention the name of Imagawa Yoshimoto again, but we do have to remember that he was surprised and defeated while conducting a head-viewing ceremony. Now I'm not suggesting that head viewing should cease, but might it be best if it were not done on the actual field of battle? The passage of time allows a degree of preparation that would otherwise be impossible. I remember being told by one of Lord Oda Nobunaga's Horse Guards how they were all invited to a drinking party for the 1573 New Year, which was to be held in Gifu Castle. The high point of the evening occurred when Lord Oda presented for their inspection the heads of the Asai and Asakura families, whom he had defeated the previous year. Each was coated in gold lacquer, and looked suitably horrible. That simply could not have been done on a battlefield.

Here a samurai presents the severed head of his enemy to his commander. The victor will be richly rewarded for his good service and the head will be returned to the victim's family.

But I digress. If you are determined to have a head-viewing *in situ* on the battlefield, and want it to be a success, then you must bear two things in mind: the first is security (which goes without saying), and the second is preparation. Fresh heads tend to ooze blood, so mount them on a spiked wooden board (make sure a supply is taken into battle) with some leaves to soak up the gore. If the fight has taken place within a castle, your maidservants can ensure that the heads are washed, the hair is combed and that a label is applied giving the name both of the deceased and of the noble samurai who has taken the trophy. The label may be attached to the pigtail.

A battlefield head-viewing ceremony should always be performed within the privacy of the field curtains. You should take your seat on the camp stool, covered with its tiger skin (I am assuming that you will one day be a general!) Next hold your fan or baton of command in your right hand, and seize the handle of your sheathed sword in the other. The trophies will then be brought to you one by one. You will be expected to examine each specimen closely, noting the expression left on the face at the moment of death, commenting upon the prowess of both victor and victim, and perhaps adding an appropriate aphorism concerning the transient nature of human existence or the impermanence of all phenomena. The brave samurai who has taken the head will deserve reward, while the brave samurai who has surrendered it will have earned your sympathy at the very least. If his death is undoubtedly tragic (for example by dying young or being the last of a noble line) then it is perfectly proper for you to weep a little, but don't overdo it. It would also perfectly acceptable for you to invite a Buddhist priest to say a few words.

Here are some examples of how heads might look when presented for inspection. Expert interpreters of yin and yang will be able to tell whether the heads are lucky or unlucky by the expressions on the faces.

The next stage is often overlooked. Having examined the heads, commented upon them and had prayers uttered, it is considered the mark of a considerate and generous victor to ensure that the heads are now handed back to the relatives of the victims. This is seldom done, which is a shame, and the example of Lord Oda Nobunaga both retaining the heads and having them gold lacquered is going a little too far in my view. It is a very firm belief within certain Buddhist traditions that a person who has gone as a Guest to the White Jade Pavilion is assured of rebirth in the Western Paradise only if his body is intact. No parts can be missing. You will become known as a good-hearted fellow if you allow Buddhist samurai such as myself to indulge our beliefs.

Don't Neglect those Rituals of Victory

Just as I placed emphasis on rituals of departure before battle, so I must insist that the rituals of victory are not overlooked in your urge to celebrate. Remember that it was the gods and Buddhas who brought you this victory, so it is very important to give thanks to them. Why not dedicate a bow or sword to the local shrine? The gesture would not go amiss. A suitable monetary donation so that pious monks may say prayers for the dead would also be most appropriate; you may even wish to order a temple to be built on the battlefield, just as His Most Illustrious Highness did at Saigadake in Hamamatsu following the most memorable battle of Mikata ga Hara in 1572. It may be that in the course of the fighting the lands or the premises of local shrines and temples have been damaged – even burned to the ground. In such cases the least you can do is to finance their complete restoration. This can prove highly expensive, as the first shogun, Minamoto Yoritomo, found when he agreed to restore the destroyed Todaiji Temple in Nara following his victory in the Gempei War of 1180–85. Did he fully appreciate that the Todaiji was the largest wooden building in the world?

I feel I should mention here the remarkable post-battle ritual performed in 1600 by the surviving samurai of Onodera Shigemichi, who perished in the flames of Nishimonai Castle. There had long been a local tradition of dancing at times of harvest and rice planting, so the samurai of Onodera danced in his memory, and have done every year since, I believe.

12
Old Age and Death

Like a fossil tree
From which we gather no flowers
Sad has been my life
Fated no fruit to produce.

DEATH POEM COMPOSED BY MINAMOTO YORIMASA
IMMEDIATELY BEFORE HIS ACT OF SEPPUKU
IN THE BYODO-IN TEMPLE OF UJI

✛ ✛ ✛

The Samurai in Old Age

In the preceding pages you have read an outline of what it takes to become a true samurai warrior, rather than one who has simply been born into that illustrious social class and cannot behave fittingly. I hope you have studied my words carefully, but I must once again stress that there is no substitute for practical experience; so join your lord in Edo, sit in when a trial is being conducted, read *Heike Monogatari*, take part in tea ceremonies and practise the martial arts at every opportunity. When you fight, fight bravely, and I will see you standing behind me at the battle of Osaka (which will most surely happen during my own lifetime, if not indeed within this present year of 1615).

It will be on such a battlefield that you achieve your destiny of becoming a real samurai, so let us imagine a battlefield where you are one of the victorious survivors. The bodies of friends and foes lie all around, but you are still alive to fight another day. Assuming that you haven't survived simply by running away, I think we can say that your duty is done. There will be many more battles to fight, I am sure, and if you have brought back a good crop of heads then an appropriate reward will be forthcoming in the shape of grants of land, promotion or both. Keep this up and who knows where you might finish your samurai career. You

When a samurai retires he can enjoy life as an administrator or might even become a great scholar and man of letters, like the modest aesthete shown in this picture.

----

may become a lord yourself one day, and run an estate wisely, perhaps even taking up a high office under His Most Excellent Highness. Like me, you may then be fortunate enough to chose a graceful retirement, have your head shaved, and continue to serve your lord in a different capacity.

Beyond that? My personal desire is that, before I become a Guest in the White Jade Pavilion, I will have returned briefly to active service and led one last attack against that rabble in Osaka Castle. I am sure that will be my final battle, and if I survive I would rather like to become a sennin. The sennin are the 'immortals', who have reached that sublime spiritual plain through meditation, asceticism and magic (powers acquired by following Taoist teachings). It will mean spending the rest of my life away from mankind in the fastness of some mountain region. Over the course of such a retreat my skin will grow white and paper-thin, and I will have a very long beard, but I think I could cope with that. In fact, I think I would make a very good sennin.

Joining Your Ancestors in the White Jade Pavilion

There will inevitably come a time when you depart this life and join your ancestors as a Guest in the White Jade Pavilion. You may have lived to an advanced age or you might have died tragically young – for who can tell the extent of his days? To die in battle is indeed honourable, but it is no less honourable to die in bed, your duty done. Even though no one can ever know the exact time of his passing, it may sometimes be that at the moment of imminent death the samurai has a choice – if not about the time of his going, then certainly about the manner. It is to this very important topic that we must now most gravely turn.

Fourteen Interesting Ways to Commit Suicide

You may have to commit suicide for any one of several reasons, and not all of them are to be welcomed; for example, you might be required to commit happy dispatch as a result of personal disgrace or dishonour. Such occasions, which are mercifully rare, are a generous alternative to being executed like a common criminal. A most unusual motive for committing suicide is to make a protest. I recall the case (which shocked everyone) of Hiraide Kiyohide, a samurai in the service of the future Lord Oda Nobunaga, who despaired at his young master's liking for debauchery and committed suicide as a way of bringing Nobunaga to his senses. This had the desired result and was commendable, if somewhat wasteful. By contrast, there is one situation similar to this that must be condemned out of hand. I mentioned it earlier, but it is so important that I must stress it once again. This is the misguided tradition of committing suicide following the death of one's lord in order to immediately join him as a Guest in the White Jade Pavilion. Nothing is more injurious to a noble house than for an heir to lose the wise counsellors and samurai who have served his father for a lifetime. This practice must never be allowed to happen.

The sole occasion when suicide is unquestionably honourable and unmistakeably meritorious occurs when a noble samurai is defeated upon the battlefield and performs happy dispatch. Cutting oneself open is a dramatic gesture, but you can become a Guest in the White Jade Pavilion using any of a number of unusual methods. All have been tried and tested by noble samurai in the past.

1 Ordinary disembowelment

This is the most common way of committing suicide on a battlefield. Known as seppuku (or by the vulgar expression hara-kiri) the technique consists of cutting open your abdomen using your dagger. If the situation permits, first withdraw from the battlefield to the seclusion of a shrine or temple. Then remove your armour, sit cross-legged, expose your abdomen and using your dagger cut open your lower belly.

Contemplate the results and die. (Be careful to lean forwards at this point. It is unseemly to be found on your back.)

This is the classic way of committing suicide. Retire to a place that ensures privacy, compose a farewell poem and cut yourself open using your dagger.

As is well known, the act of seppuku is often performed with the assistance of a second. This loyal friend, who must be an expert swordsman, stands beside you as you perform the act. At the precise moment that you plunge the dagger into your abdomen, he will deliver a single blow with his sword, cutting off your head. This renders seppuku much less painful. The most skilled and devoted seconds will cut so deftly and precisely as to leave a small flap of skin between the head and one of the shoulders. Your head will not then bounce along the ground, which would be considered most unseemly.

The practice of ritual disembowelment is rendered less painful by the intervention of a second, who will cut your head off at the exact moment you make the final incision.

2 Disembowelment with poetry

As with number 1, but before making the final incision a poem is composed on an appropriate theme. If no paper is available, write the poem on your war fan. Such an act was performed in 1180 by Minamoto Yorimasa at the Byodo-In Temple following his defeat at the battle of Uji, and was regarded as most honourable. Poems written under these circumstances are usually quite short.

3 Disembowelment with poetry written in one's own blood

This is a nice variation on number 2. To take the blood from one's own carved abdomen after the incision has been made undeniably lends the act an extra cachet. Otherwise, inscribing the poem upon a temple door using blood from a wound before committing suicide may be regarded as equally praiseworthy and much less messy. Akechi Mitsuyoshi managed to combine both methods in 1582 and wrote a poem on a temple door using blood from the final incision before expiring, which was quite an achievement.

Here we see the noble suicide of Akechi Mitsuyoshi, who wrote a farewell poem on a temple door using blood from the incision he had made to disembowel himself.

4 Falling on your sword

This is a quick and easy method when you are hard pressed on the battlefield and the situation does not allow you to withdraw to a place of repose. It is less honourable than numbers 1–3, and has the unfortunate association of being the method chosen by the female defenders of Tsuneyama Castle in 1577. To be remembered by future generations as the samurai who 'did it like a girl' may not be acceptable to many warriors.

5 Falling forwards from horse, sword in mouth

This method, performed most memorably by Imai Kanehira at the battle of Awazu in 1184, is both effective and dramatic. Keep your teeth clenched. Frozen ground helps.

This is the dramatic suicide of Imai Kanehira at the battle of Awazu in 1184.
He jumped headfirst from his horse, sword in mouth.

----

6 Falling forwards from castle tower, sword in mouth

This remarkable variation on number 5 was performed by Matsunaga Kojiro at the siege of Shikizan Castle in 1577. His father Matsunaga Hisahide had just committed suicide using method 1, so Kojiro cut off his father's head and leaped to his own death with his sword in his mouth and the head in his hands. Incidentally, prior to his suicide, Matsunaga Hisahide had smashed a priceless tea bowl so that it would not fall into the hands of his enemies. (See 'The Tea Ceremony – Dos and Don'ts' in chapter 7).

Matsunaga Kojiro committed suicide at the siege of Shikizan Castle in 1577 by jumping from the castle tower with his sword in his mouth and carrying his father's severed head in his hands.

----

7 Headlong dash into the midst of enemies against a hail of arrows

Why kill yourself when the enemy can do it for you? This method is quick and extremely dramatic, as illustrated by the successful suicidal charge of the Kusunoki brothers into a volley of deadly arrows at the battle of Shijo-Nawate in 1348. You will be left looking like a porcupine, which will bring great honour upon your ancestors. It is, however, important to note that this method may not be totally effective. The approach of a furious samurai intent on death may cause the enemy to shoot wide or even run away, as happened when Shibata Katsuie led a suicidal charge out of the gates of Chokoji Castle in 1570. In this case he survived, won the battle, was richly rewarded and went on to become a renowned general.

8 Headlong dash into the midst of enemies against a hail of bullets

Yamamoto Kansuke's death at the fourth battle of Kawanakajima in 1561 is the classic example, and if it was good enough for Takeda Shingen's finest general then it is quite good enough for you, so don't moan about the fact that the fatal bullets are being fired by lewd and sordid persons.

They would not be firing if you were not there. Besides, the order to fire will have been given by someone of a rank equivalent to your own, so don't automatically turn this method down.

9 Drowning whilst being weighed down by one's armour

Sea battles add the exciting prospect of death by drowning. There are several instances in Japanese history of successful suicides at sea, but take note that nowadays many suits of armour are made predominantly from leather, and therefore have a tendency to float. Also, if you belong to a clan such as the Aizu, which has a great tradition of swimming while wearing armour, your natural tendency to survive or even to show off your skills may mean you forget the original purpose of your immersion.

10 Drowning whilst being weighed down by an anchor

The famous instance is Taira Tomomori at the battle of Dannoura in 1185. It really doesn't get much better than this, particularly when you haunt the locality for centuries to come. (See 'Ghosts and Other Strange Beings' in chapter 6.)

11 Drowning whilst weighed down by a temple bell

The unusual death of the wife of the keeper of Sakasai Castle, which occurred when the castle fell to the Hojo, was exceedingly honourable. She simply slipped the temple bell that was used for signalling over her shoulders and toppled into the castle pond.

12 Cutting off one's own head

This is technically so difficult, requiring both a *very* sharp blade and an intimate knowledge of human anatomy, that there are only two known examples in the whole of Japanese history. The first was Nitta Yoshisada at the battle of Fujishima in 1338. Yoshisada's horse was felled by an arrow, trapping him beneath it. Being unable to reach his abdomen, Yoshisada cut off his own head. That in itself is so remarkable that the variation of the story that has him performing the act then standing and continuing to fight may be dismissed as fanciful. Many years later,

Miura Yoshimoto cut his own head off when the castle of Arai fell to Hojo Soun in 1510. It was very messy.

There are only two recorded instances in Japanese history of samurai committing suicide by cutting off their own heads. This picture shows Miura Yoshimoto decapitating himself at the siege of Arai in 1510.

----

13 Starving oneself to death

Starving oneself is difficult and undramatic, although we had a recent example during the winter campaign at Osaka in 1614, when Yabe Toranosuke did so in his mortification at having arrived too late for the battle.

Here we see the tragic and pitiful sight of two defeated samurai on the battlefield. One lies dead while the other makes an attempt to rise.

----

14 Being buried alive

Sometimes embarrassment is justified and can provide a positive result. In 1290 (or thereabouts) Shibuya Shigechika failed to overcome his enemy, and so had himself buried alive, fully armoured and mounted on his horse.

What Will Happen When I Am Dead?

You are now dead.

Your corpse lies on the battlefield, a pathetic yet noble sight. You may have lost your head, but if your enemy is generous then it will be reunited with your body in the very near future. As you lie there, priests will pass near by, intoning prayers for you. These brave men actually do this while the battle is still raging, and when all is quiet your fellow samurai, with tears streaming from their eyes, will carry your body from the battlefield.

Regardless of whether you have committed suicide or been killed by the enemy, there now begins a very long and very important process: your soul must be successfully steered to the Western Paradise, a process that depends upon the actions performed by your surviving family. The first requirement is for your soul to be firmly separated from your body. Because of the painful and tragic way in which you probably met your end this is by no means straightforward, and I will deal later with the serious consequences that can arise when the soul is not correctly separated.

There will soon be a funeral for your corpse, which will be cremated and the ashes interred in a grave. Sometimes this will be done on the battlefield where you fell. The funeral (as is the case for the whole process in fact) will be in the hands of Buddhist clergy, whose prayers and services will ensure that your soul is freed within 49 days of your death. Shinto priests will have nothing to do with death. Shinto is about life. Buddhism is about death.

A Buddhist priest or monk, probably one from your local temple, will then take your sorrowing family a temporary ihai (funerary tablet). On the 49th day after your death this will be replaced with the final version, a black lacquered tablet on which your posthumous name is written in gold. This tablet will be kept and displayed in the butsudan (Buddhist altar) in your home, where your wife and children will revere it for many years to come.

Your first Bon Festival as a spirit will come around within a year of your death. At Bon you, and the spirits of all your ancestors, will return to the family home. Your soul is now truly free, and over the next 33 years it will make the long, slow journey to Paradise, helped on its way by the actions of your surviving family (without whose prayers the soul may become lost). At the end of this time, when it is likely no living memory of you remains, the ihai will be taken back to the temple and placed on a shelf in an inner chapel.

You are now a god. You may even have been enshrined at your local Shinto sanctuary so that you can be worshipped within your particular locality – but whatever happens, you are now also that most wonderful of things: an ancestor. In China people literally worship their ancestors. In Japan we don't go quite that far, but you will be honoured, and your deeds will be written and sung about in the centuries to come. In these ways your descendants will remember you, and by returning to them every Bon Festival you will never cease to play a part in your household, even long after you have gone. Otherwise you are happy as a Guest in the White Jade Pavilion of Heaven.

A successful samurai – like this veteran, skilled in the way of the bow – would have served his lord time and time again before death.

- - - - - - - - -

Angry Ghosts and How to Placate Them

But what happens to those souls who have no descendants to pray for them? Others can supplicate on their behalf, of course, and myriad are the offerings and sutras issued by worthy priests for their unfortunate souls. Yet sometimes, sadly, the process does not work and they remain as troubled spirits. How do we know? Because out of nowhere come famines, floods and typhoons to devastate the land. These events are the actions of onryo (angry ghosts), who, being yet possessed of the unruly passion with which they died, vent their anger on the world of living men. Fortunately, there is a way to control them, which is to instate them as gods in a Shinto shrine. In time they will be placated, but the process must be continued and never neglected, lest their wrath break out again. Examples of onryo include the courtier Sugawara Michizane, a man of honour who was most cruelly and unjustly executed because of the false rumours brought against him. His angry spirit sought terrible revenge, causing crops to fail and animals to die; but wise men enshrined him, and he is now safely worshipped as Tenjin, the god of learning.

So honour your ancestors and perform rituals for them, because they depend on you as much as you depend on the example they have set – and none of us is exempt from the certainty of death. I also have to face the fact that I will not survive, and may perhaps leave my corpse upon the battlefield. I know what will happen to my physical body, but what of my spirit? Will my descendants honour me? This is certainly to be expected. In fact my son has already assured me that he has selected a plot beside Umawatari Castle for the construction of a temple in my memory, to be known as the Bogyuji. There, pious monks will offer prayers for the repose of my soul. Finally, I may also expect to be established as a god within the ancient Umawatari Shrine beside the Mukiwata River, where I will enjoy an annual festival. How pleasant is the thought that those simple farmers of Hitachi province will think of me as they tuck into their octopus balls! I have so much to look forward to when I am dead – thanks to my adoring family and their prayers. And if they don't do all this, I will simply come back and haunt them.

In conclusion, young samurai, follow the example of your ancestors but, follow too the words written in this book. You will then become the glorious samurai warrior that it is your rightful inheritance to be.

Umawatari Bogyu

Lord of Hitachi and Grand Chamberlain to
His Most Excellent Highness the Shogun

Epilogue

by Stephen Turnbull

✢ ✢ ✢

As I am sure you will have guessed, Umawatari Bogyu is a fictional character, whose life and personality I have based on several real-life advisors to the first Tokugawa shoguns. Despite this, I am convinced we can imagine him presenting the manuscript of *Buke Monogatari* to Tokugawa Hidetada before riding off with his master to take part in the siege of Osaka Castle in the summer of 1615. This was indeed the final showdown with the Toyotomi family, and it ended in a major encounter known as the battle of Tennoji, when the defenders took the risk of riding out of the castle to engage the besieging Tokugawa. After the shogun overcame them, he ordered a massive bombardment of the keep, and the Tokugawa army closed in on the doomed castle, and those who had remained inside.

The Tokugawa victory was to ensure their dominance over Japan for the next two and a half centuries. As for those who perished at Osaka, they were remembered in exactly the same way as our fictional grand chamberlain envisaged for himself: their ashes interred in local Buddhist temples, their spirits enshrined in the local Shinto shrines and their memories forever reawakened by the wind blowing through the grass on the sites of long-abandoned castles.

The crossed-feathers mon of the
Asano family of Hiroshima and Ako.

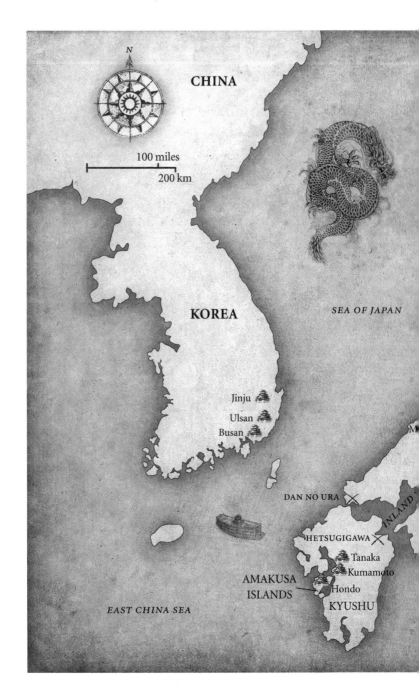

CHINA

N

100 miles
200 km

KOREA

SEA OF JAPAN

Jinju
Ulsan
Busan

M

DAN NO URA

INLAND

HETSUGIGAWA

Tanaka
Kumamoto

AMAKUSA
ISLANDS

Hondo

KYUSHU

EAST CHINA SEA

TOHOKU

Omori

Nishimonai

JAPAN

KAWANAKAJIMA

FUJISHIMA

IGAHARA   KURIKARA

ike Biwa

yoto

nimi

Numata

Sakasai

KANTO

Kawagoe

Edo (Tokyo)

Gifu

HONSHU

Kamakura

ttori

ayama

Arai

Odawara

KOKU

Mt. Fuji

MINATOGAWA

NAGASHINO

NAGAKUTE

Muraki

Anotsu

OKEHAZAMA

UJI

YAMAZAKI

Osaka

INATOGAWA

PACIFIC OCEAN

Glossary

ashigaru foot soldier

bakufu the shogunate

bokken wooden practice sword

budo martial arts

bugei techniques of the martial arts

bushido the Way of the Warrior

daimyo Japanese warlord

do body armour

dojo martial arts practice hall

dojo yaburi contests between schools, or external challenges for gain

gunkimono the war tales

hatamoto a daimyo's closest retainers

kabuto helmet

kamayari a cross-bladed spear

kami deity of the Shinto religion

kata set forms of swordplay

kengo master swordsman

kenjutsu sword-fighting techniques

koku a measure of wealth expressed in rice

kote sleeve armour

kyuba no michithe way of horse and bow

kyudo Japanese archery

machi bugyo magistrate

maku field curtains on a battlefield

naginata a glaive (polearm) with a curved blade

ninja secret spies and assassins

ninjutsu the art of stealth and invisibility

otokodate townsmen 'samurai'

ronin a samurai without a master to serve

ryu school of swordsmanship

sake rice wine

samurai a member of the military class

sensei teacher

shikoro neck guard

shogun the military dictator of Japan

sode shoulder plates

sohei warrior monks

tengu forest goblin

tsumeru pulling a blow

yabusame horseback archery

yamabushi a mountain ascetic

yari spear

yarijutsu spear-fighting techniques

yoroi armour worn by high-ranking samurai

Timeline

Further Reading

If you think the florid language I have put into the mouth of Umawatari Bogyu is exaggerated, then there are two books that will confirm that in many ways I have acted with some restraint. A. L. Sadler's classic *The Maker of Modern Japan* (London, 1937), a biography of Tokugawa Ieyasu ('His Most Illustrious Highness'), reproduces perfectly the honorific language of Tokugawa Japan, and for an authentic account of the intrigue and mayhem in the courts of the early Tokugawa shoguns you can do no better than read Beatrice Bodart-Bailey's *The Dog Shogun* (Honolulu, 2006), a life of Tokugawa Tsunayoshi.

Apart from Bogyu himself, all the details of battles, armour, weapons and daily life are authentic, and may be followed up in several of my own works, as well as in books by other authors. If you want to know more about the martial arts, my book *The Samurai Swordsman* (Oxford and New York, 2008) is a good starting point, while *Strongholds of the Samurai* (Oxford and New York, 2009) is a comprehensive guide to Japanese castles. For female warriors, read my *Samurai Women* (Oxford and New York, 2010), and for the wonderful world of Japanese religion try *The Samurai and the Sacred* (Oxford and New York, 2006). I have also produced several monographs in the Osprey *Campaigns* Series on certain battles mentioned briefly here, such as *Nagashino 1575*; *Kawanakajima 1553–64*; *Osaka 1615*; *The Mongol Invasions of Japan 1274 and 1281*; and *The Samurai Capture a King: Okinawa 1609*, as well as many other titles listed on my website (www.stephenturnbull.com).

To learn more about the yamabushi and the rich world of folk religion, read Carmen Blacker's wonderful book *The Catalpa Bow* (London, 1975); while books by the eminent scholars William Wayne Farris, Karl Friday and Thomas Conlan will tell you much about the samurai of an earlier age.

Sources of Quotations

Page 12

'The special dispensation of our Imperial Land …'
Motoori Norinaga, *On the Emperor and Japan*, 1790

Page 32

'The Way of the Samurai is found in death.'
Nabeshima Tsunetomo, *Hidden Among Leaves*, 1710

Page 45

'When he goes forth to war the soldier is prepared …'
Hayakawa Kyukei, from the preface to *The Manufacture of Armour and Helmets*, 1799

Page 54

'The sword is the soul of the samurai.'
Tokugawa Ieyasu, *Precepts*, 1616

Page 67

'It is clearly written in the Four Books and the Five Classics …'
Imagawa Ryoshun, *Regulations*, 1412

Page 76

'Above all, believe in the gods and Buddhas.'
Hojo Soun, *Twenty-One Precepts*, c. 1500

Page 91

'One should put forth effort in matters of learning.'
Kato Kiyomasa, *Precepts*, c. 1610

Page 102

'There is a saying of the ancients that goes …'
Takeda Nobushige, *Opinions in Ninety-Nine Articles*, 1558

Page 115

'Having been born into the house of a warrior …'
Kato Kiyomasa, *Precepts*, c. 1610

Page 148

'I sincerely assure you that of all the palaces and houses …'
Luís Fróis, SJ, on visiting Gifu Castle

Page 160

'After the battle, tighten the cords of your helmet.'
Tokugawa Teyasu, speaking at the Battle of Sekigahara, 1600

Page 165

'Like a fossil tree …'
Death poem composed by Minamoto Yorimasa immediately before his act of seppuku in the Byodo-in Temple of Uji, 1180

List of Illustrations

Pages 81, 88
Utagawa Kuniyoshi, prints from the series *Teiheiki Eiyûden* (Heroic Stories of the Taiheiki) 1848–49, private collection

Pages 82–83
Detail from a modern reproduction of the a screen in Osaka Castle, private collection

Page 84
Utagawa Toyonobu, woodblock print from the series *Shinsen Taikoki*, 1883, private collection

Page 85
From a modern copy of a painted screen in Hikone Castle Museum, *c.* 1635, private collection

Pages 86–87
Kobayashi Kiyochika, woodblock print of Emperor Go-Daigo and his general Kusunoki Masashige, 1877, private collection

Woodblock prints *passim* are taken from the author's collection.

All photographs (pages 137–44) by Stephen Turnbull, except a samurai swimming (page 139), from a photograph in Kumamoto castle, by kind permission.

Index

Page numbers in *italics* refer to illustrations and captions